RESILIENT LOVING

A Practical Compass for Partners of People on the Autism Spectrum

A little book to top up your hope, guide you, and inspire you

Mabel Schenone

CONTENTS

INTRODUCTION

Hello, dear reader! Are you wondering whether this book is for you? Let's find out.

Are you in a relationship with somebody who you suspect or know is on the autism spectrum?

Do you sometimes find the relationship tough and very different from what other couples seem to go through?

Do you feel confused as to whether you are in a healthy relationship or whether you should leave it?

Sometimes we have tried our best to accommodate our partner's idiosyncrasies and needs. Sometimes we have adapted to such an extent that we don't really know what we need and what we want any more. Sometimes we just don't know who we are any more.

If you recognise your situation in some of the above, the first part of this book will be especially helpful for you.

If you feel OK in yourself but want to improve the way you relate to your autistic dear one, the second part of this book will be really helpful for you.

Whatever your circumstances, please take all the time you need to interact with the material in this book. Feel free to pause, feel, and reflect as you go along. This book is meant to take you by the hand along a gentle, progressive journey in which you may discover new things and blind spots. It is also meant as a resource you can pick up when you feel a bit down, or lost.

I wonder what you would tell me if we were sharing a cup of tea and a chat. I am sure you would have plenty to say! There can be pain and loneliness in the relationship. There is little reciprocity and we can easily get emotionally exhausted. Communication can feel like a mine-field.

Sometimes, there are plenty of positive aspects and the relationship can be saved. Sometimes there are many incompatible factors or some personality traits or disorders due to which it may be wiser and safer to end the relationship.

No matter what the circumstances and what our future may be like, I have experienced over and over that we can transform the suffering and have a much better relationship with ourselves and with our partners.

It is my sincere wish that you will find your way to deal with your unique combination of circumstances and reconnect with peace, strength and love, while setting up the relationship for success if you decide to continue in it.

This little book is meant as a series of stepping stones in the direction you would like your life with your partner to go. As long as you continue with the explorations it suggests, it will get you the results you want to experience.

You can follow the order in which the topics are presented or jump to a point that catches your attention. However, I would recommend you spend some time on Part One before continuing with Part Two. This will help you find some inspiration to get you back into a more loving, vibrant you first.

Of course, if one day you are reading or practising any of the suggested activities and you feel increasing tension, resistance or any significant unpleasant feeling, be compassionate with yourself and stop. You may need to move your body a little, or to feel what you are experiencing in an accepting manner and see what happens. You may need to put the book down altogether and do something else for now. You may be about to discover an important clue to an emotional bruise from the past, so please be gentle with yourself.

If I were advising my younger self on what main tools to pack in her backpack for the special part of her marriage, I would recommend to her three kinds of tools:

1. Self-care tools to support her in re-connecting with the most vibrant part of herself;

2. Knowledge tools to discover as much as she can about autism; and

3. Awareness of her partner tools so that she can get to know and connect with the specific person she is dating/lives with/has married.

So this book follows that path.

In Part One, you will find a compilation of self-care tools I have gathered along the way... or created especially for you and me. Even though they are simple, some of them require digging deep into what we really think, feel or want. Take your time and allow them to systematically lead you along a journey of reconnecting with yourself at your best by providing hope, relief, or inspiration. This first part is mostly about you because it is my experience that when I meet somebody else who is in a relationship with an autistic person, initially they want to be listened to, seen, validated, and understood. I will also add a few personal examples from my life, but Part One is mainly for you to connect with yourself. Some of the tools I propose in Part One may seem more serious and others are definitely playful, so you can choose the right tool to suit your mood and what is happening in your life. So Part One of the book relates to the first item I would advise my younger self to pack on her backpack for the relationship.

The second item relates to learning about autism. The list of resources on autism would be endless. If you are a bookworm like me, in the UK, Jessica Kingsley Publishers has an incredible selection. Of course, there is also Mr Google. Don't forget YouTube. There are also many films about autism, including Life, Animated (2016), El Faro de las Orcas (The Lighthouse of the Whales, also known as A Place to Dream) (2016), and Temple Grandin (2010).

Having said that, throughout the book I will incorporate some of the things I have learned about autism in general during my never-ending journey of trying to gain more awareness of what my husband's reality may be like.

In Part Two, you will find some musings around autistic traits that may be at play in our relationship, with an emphasis on those that affect communication.

Since **no two people on the autistic spectrum are the same**, I don't think it is possible to offer one size that fits all. In this section, I will reveal everyday examples from my marriage. You will get to know what I mean by gaining "awareness of your partner" (the third item I would advise my younger self to pack in her backpack). You will also get to know me (and my husband) a bit better. I will tell you about the things I find most challenging and how I navigate them. Pick and choose what seems relevant to you. Stay curious. Try things for size. Adapt what seems to fit. It is your journey.

Let me share something right from the start: I am a great believer in groups. I have found that a support group for partners like us is an invaluable source of empathic validation, knowledge, connection, and emotional renewal. If you find one that matches your circumstances, I would recommend you stick to it no matter what. It can be a lifeline if you are struggling or when, after a period of denial of how autism affects you and your relationship, suddenly your partner has or meltdown that rocks your world again.

Of course, your personal circumstances may require professional advice. If so, please make sure the therapist you work with is at the very least autism-informed, otherwise, the work you do may be perfect but impossible to apply in your situation.

Similarly, even though I have tried to make the text as inclusive as possible and it is not intended to leave out any sexual orientation or gender, autism traits in men do not present themselves in exactly the same way as in women, so some of the aspects of this book may need adapting to your personal circumstances in terms of gender differences, too.

A little background information about my husband and me. We have been married for over 30 years and, believe me, our marriage could have ended on so many occasions! It's been very difficult many times. We have separated several times. I left him and lived abroad for a few years about 20 years ago. Even now, our relationship continues to have ups and downs, but instead of drifting apart, we somehow find ways to stay connected. Sometimes connection may take the form of resting a foot on my husband's while we eat in silence and holding hands in bed at night when that is all he can cope with because his anxiety is near meltdown level or I am hurting because of something that happened that day.

I know from my own experience that what you will read in this book works.

The universal and very simple tools that seem to help us

-no matter what the situation may be- are: 1) to keep as calm as possible and 2) to stay curious (which in turn engages those parts of the brain that help us to calm down).

In order to be able to use these two tools systematically in our relationship, we need to feel strong, energised, and empowered. Everything I share in this book has helped me to get there.

It would be impossible for my husband and I to connect if I didn't keep my level of emotional energy high enough. I know the way to do that.

Will you join me on this journey so that you too can take steps towards feeling the way you want to feel in your relationship? I take this journey quite seriously, but as you will see, I can get playful, too.

The only requirement is that you are willing to keep or develop an open mind and a growth mindset.

Before we start our journey, I would like to remind you that apart from this book you are getting The Companion, which has plenty of space for you to reflect and keep any new insights, discoveries and tools.

In several parts of this book, you will see images of a

More at
The Companion

treasure chest like this one ⬚. They are invitations for you to head to your copy of The Companion. If you haven't got your copy of The Companion yet, download it for free, in Word format so that you can add your thoughts, fill in charts and/

or more pages as necessary, from https://
resilientloving.co.uk/index.php?
controller=attachment&id_attachment=10

Another signpost in this book is the following:

◆ ◆ ◆

If you don't see that separator, keep going because the
section continues on the next page.

◆ ◆ ◆

PART 1: EMOTIONAL SELF-CARE

You may have experienced difficult moments in your relationship or heard somebody else speak about theirs.

You may have seen research about the negative effects of being in a relationship with somebody on the autism spectrum.

We may feel insignificant and powerless. However, this is not the truth. It is a perception, and we can change such unhelpful perceptions easily, one by one, so that we can remember our own significance and power.

Do you feel that the way you behave and feel in the relationship is currently defining who you are? I am sure that nobody would ever allow a relationship to define who they are consciously or deliberately, but when things are not going well it certainly feels as if that's all there is to us.

As a result of our experiences, right now we may be feeling...

What would your own list include?

More at
The Companion Go ahead and write down your list, you will find space for this at The Companion. **You might want to revisit your list after you have completed this journey to confirm what aspects have already changed for you.**

I know that it is easier said than done for many of us to stay as calm, happy, grounded, and rested as possible because we are caring individuals. That is why we will use this book as a guide to get to where we want to be.

The way we relate to ourselves informs the way we relate to others

In my experience, many partners of people with autism are very caring. However, we tend to care for everybody except ourselves. Eventually, we feel depleted and we start treating others the way we treat ourselves.

That is why we will start our journey with some tools for self-care. You can add a cup of tea, a candlelit bubble bath or any other self-care tip you already know. My intention is to nourish your creativity with some less common ideas.

As our destination is achieving a resilient loving attitude, let's explore some aspects of resilience.

What do you think resilience means?

Do you think resilience is a desirable goal for yourself and the way you relate to others, including your partner/spouse?

Do you feel you have to make do with the amount of resilience you were born with or do you think it can be developed?

Do you feel it is too late for you? If so, can you ask yourself this question: 'If not now, when?'

The word "resilience" evokes many things, such as flexibility, adaptability and strength.

Resilience involves:

> The capacity to face stress or adversity without compromising our values;

> The ability to think and behave with some degree of rationality even under pressure or to come back to a state of equanimity fairly soon;

> A sense of integrity and moral strength;

> A long-term perspective of life;

> The strength to adapt to difficult situations while continuing to function;

> Healthy habits;

> The ability to recover from a challenging event or circumstance with new skills; and

> The strength of mind and character that allows us to survive despite adversity.

Resilience is a skill that helps our mental, emotional, physical, social, environmental, and spiritual wellbeing.

As with any other skill, it can be practised and expanded so that we remain calmer and enjoy life more fully. Resilience also helps us to reduce the risk of stress-related conditions or to recover from them.

In my experience, we need a fair amount of resilience to enjoy life.
We also need resilience to love and to be in a relationship with somebody who processes life, thinks, feels, and communicates in a very different way from ours.

The word "loving" in the title of this little book points to the fact that love is not a concept or feeling that remains static, but rather an ever-changing experience in action. Our loving capacity and attitude can be practised and renewed. Let's start!

SELF-CARE TOOL #1: LEARNING NEW THINGS

I would like to invite you to reflect on your attitude towards learning new things, and then, perhaps, take a leap of faith and learn something new or a new way of doing something.

More at
The Companion   Your Companion includes this tool too, so that you can record your answers.

What is something you do especially well?

How do you know that you do it so well?

How did you learn to do it? Did you take formal lessons or was it informal learning? Did you learn with others or was it solo learning? Did you learn mainly through reading/listening/watching videos or through practice? Did you learn through trial and error?

What is something you can't do or haven't done well?

How do you know you can't do it/don't do it well?

How could you learn to do it/or learn to do it better?

Will you give it a try?

SELF-CARE TOOL #2: OUR EMOTIONAL CLIMATE

How are you feeling right now? Like a raging volcano? Like a warm, private beach? Like a choppy sea? Like a calm meadow in full bloom? Like a smooth-flowing stream of water? Like a downpour? Like the calm before a storm? Like the eye of a tornado? Or maybe you have no idea how you are feeling?

It may be helpful to consider our experience along two main variables: one is its intensity and the other one is its quality.

We can rate our emotional intensity at any given moment by using a simple colour spectrum, like the one below:

LOW INTENSITY	LOW INCREASING	NEUTRAL, BALANCED	INCREASING	HIGH INTENSITY

The quality can range from PLEASANT to UNPLEASANT. Here is an example.

The scales may vary from person to person, and perhaps from day to day.

For some people, their starting point may be being content and their most unpleasant experience may be apathy or a panic attack.

For others, the scale may start at disappointment and go down to resentment, and yet for others, the scale may start at being ok and go up to unbridled joy.

It can be immensely useful to start considering our emotions along these lines. Sometimes we don't really know how we are feeling, but once we start putting our attention on the two variables of intensity and pleasantness, we may start getting clues as to what is going on.

We may also start discovering patterns such as "I tend to feel a high intensity emotion when I am around my partner. Sometimes it is pleasant, sometimes it is neutral and sometimes it is very unpleasant."

If you want, you can use the scales of intensity and pleasantness on their own as above. I like combining them on a chart and adding further details.

Below is an example of a chart of my most visited emotional states, where I have also divided the experience into what happens in the emotions and what happens in the body.

	PLEASANT	UNPLEASANT
HIGH EMOTIONAL INTENSITY	inspired	irritated
LOW EMOTIONAL INTENSITY	calm	lonely
HIGH PHYSICAL INTENSITY	energised	tense
LOW PHYSICAL INTENSITY	relaxed	exhausted

SELF-CARE TOOL #3: FROM INTENTIONS TO ACTION...

We all experience times when we make great plans but then fail to implement them. We may forget them, we may cancel them, we may dread them or we may decide to leave them for another time.

If this is creating tension or causing problems in our lives, we can explore what stands in our way and how motivated we are.

So let's identify the factors that may be stopping us.

More at
The Companion

It may help to think about a concrete situation we want to avoid, such as putting off checking our bank balance, making an appointment with our dentist, or making a change in our lives:

What is hindering your progress towards doing that?

Who might be upset if you couldn't be as available as before because of your focus on your task or goal?

Who might be upset if you completed this task?

Why can't you complete this task?

Because I am (not)....

What fear (or other feeling you consider undesirable) is there around completing this task?

What do you actually feel when you think about completing the task?

Can you find any other reason for delaying/not doing this?

Now that we have a clearer picture of what we may be trying to avoid, it would be beneficial to start thinking about the positive things we might gain if we overcame the hindrances and went ahead. These are factors that will help us to feel motivated:

How will you feel when you complete that task?

Who will be most proud of you for completing this task?

(The answer may be "Me" and that's all right, too).

What positive reasons for completing the task soon can you think of?

Is it safe for you to complete the task?

Is it the right time for you to complete the task? If not, can you foresee the right time to do it within the next few days/weeks/months?

If you decide to postpone it, can you commit to completing it by a certain date, without procrastinating it again and again?

SELF-CARE TOOL #4: EMOTIONAL MANAGEMENT

I am sure you are a strong person in many ways, but I also have good reasons to believe you are a human being. So there will probably be times when emotions surface inside you. Some may make you feel raw and vulnerable. It is easy to be in the habit of not wanting to feel those because we fear we might lose our strength.

However, emotions are useful signs, like a popup on our computer alerting us about something. The problem is not the emotion itself. The suffering, and maybe even illness, comes from how we manage our emotions, the things we do with them or the things we do to avoid them.

Even if you feel that emotions manage you, rather than the other way around, please join me in this exploration anyhow.

Let's try to take an inventory of our current emotion management toolkit - hopefully this will change after reading this!

We may manage our emotions by using defence tools in an attempt to feel stronger inside so that we can counter them, deny them, repress them, forget them or do anything other than feel them. These tools imply a movement away from emotions.

Below you will find a list of examples of such tools we pick up when we don't want to feel what we are feeling. I would recommend taking some time to reflect on those that sound familiar:

CRITICISING OR BLAMING OTHERS: Focussing our attention on somebody else in this way helps us to we feel some sense of power (we think we are better, we know better or we do better than the person or thing we are criticising) and focuses our attention on something other than our emotional states.

CRITICISING OR BLAMING OURSELVES: Focussing our attention on ourselves in a negative way helps us feel stronger because we can control what our inner critical voice focuses on. On the other hand, we focus our attention on an alleged defect or wrongdoing rather than our emotional states. It may feel safer than vulnerability.

RAGING: This is usually a form of misplaced anger, such as when we lash out at our partners when in fact, we are frustrated because of something that has happened at work.

DENYING: We may change the subject so that we don't even need to think about it. Or we may roll our eyes, diffuse emotions by using sarcasm, jokes, or smiles.

BEHAVING IN AN ENTITLED MANNER: Assuming a grandiose stance in which we feel we are superior. In this way, we get to justify our emotions instead of feeling them and we act while in an emotionally aroused state.

BARGAINING: We engage in bargaining when we think along the lines of "if I do this, the emotion will disappear". Sometimes bargaining takes the form of constant apologising.

ENGAGING IN ADDICTIVE BEHAVIOURS/DISTRACTIONS: These are things we do in the hope of numbing our emotions, behaviours in which we engage even though they may potentially have a negative effect on our lives. We are seeking to reduce or eliminate the emotions in the present, even if we are aware of the negative consequences in the future, such as when we go on an unnecessary shopping spree, work too much, eat unhealthy food, etc.

OBSESSING: Ruminating endlessly about events (asking why or replaying the story by thinking "he said... and I said..." over and over, etc.) instead of exploring the meaning those events have for us and the accompanying feelings and emotions.

LOOKING FOR ACTION: The opposite of being stuck is taking action, so trying to do something may feel better than the emotional state itself, but acting while we are under the influence of strong emotions may not yield the results we want.

COLLAPSING: Feeling exhausted, procrastinating, not talking to anybody, avoiding social contact, spacing out, or day-dreaming. This usually happens after we have been holding it together over an extended period of time. There comes a point in which we can't cope any longer and we just check out from our usual activities or from the things we know will be helpful.

By the way, the idea is to take an honest look inside the toolkit, not to sort them into good or bad tools. You can sharpen and put your tools back or replace any you are not too happy with. The choice is always yours. This is a judgement-free zone.

Feel free to add your own to the list. Enjoy!

In some cases, these may well be the best option.

When you become aware that you have picked up one of these tools, if on reflection you realise it would be better to put it down, instead of resisting it, suppressing it, or looking for a distraction, try to recognise it. You may name it by thinking "Oh, oh. Here I am obsessing about what happened again." Secondly, drop into your body (How does this feel in my body?). You may already notice a shift by this stage. We will add further steps later.

Below, you will find other tools you may want to add to your repertoire of emotion management responses.

We may manage our emotions in a more welcoming way by:

ACCEPTING: Adopting a curious stance and exploring what is going on. We may need to take time out from others in order to do it fully. It is not easy to accept unpleasant emotions, so it is good to be gentle with ourselves and to be mindful of our experience. Sometimes acceptance may mean saying to ourselves 'I am willing to accept that a part of me is feeling... right now' or 'I am willing to accept that I am struggling to accept this feeling right now.'

NAMING: Naming the emotion helps the more rational part of our brain to get engaged and 'come to the rescue', as it were. If we cannot really give the emotion a name, we may express it as closely as possible through movement, choosing a song that reflects it or an image that symbolises it, etc. For instance, we could use SELF-CARE TOOL #2: Our emotional climate to help us to express it.

FEELING THE RAW EMOTION: Usually raw emotions feel as if they are at a deeper level. They may not be the first thing we can name. For instance, you may think 'I feel disappointed', but on closer inspection you may realise that there is something else underneath the disappointment. For instance, you may discover that you fear not being important to your partner. There are not too many raw emotions, perhaps just the following six: fear, anger, sadness, disgust, joy, and excitement.

FEELING THE EMOTION IN OUR BODY: Are we feeling cold or heated? Where is the emotional charge? Is it static or moving? Is its intensity changing in any way? Can we give it a colour? Can we rate it on a scale from 1 to 10?

TRYING TO UNDERSTAND THE MESSAGE EMOTIONS BRING: What do we need at this moment? Do we long for something?

Have you already got any of these tools in your toolkit? Have you got any more that work well for you? Again, feel free to add your own because they open an important new perspective.

When we are in pain or stressed, the tendency is to run away from our painful emotions or to run toward something we see as more desirable. We are not comfortable in the present, so we run away from it and either revisit the past or run into the future and imagine that if some circumstances change, then and only then, we will finally be happy.

The reality is that running away from our experience or running towards an experience we consider better than the one we are having has no long-term positive consequences.

We are not there for ourselves. When we are not there for ourselves, we can't take care of ourselves.

When we are not there for ourselves, we can't be there for others, either.

When we run away from ourselves, we also run away from our dear ones. No wonder we feel lonely and tired!

The second -more welcoming- set of tools we have explored helps us stop running. We can then be there with whatever is happening and stay calmer, more curious, compassionate, connected, confident, and clear.

If you realise your current first choice is not the tools from the second set, why don't you choose one now and commit to applying it for a week to see what happens?

SELF-CARE TOOL #5: BALANCE, BALANCE, BALANCE!

We all know about the importance of having balance in our lives. The kind of relationship we are in usually lacks reciprocity, so we may end up giving much more than we are getting in some areas. I would like to invite you to make sure as many other aspects of your life as possible are in balance.

More at
The Companion Warm-up activity: Let's start by imagining a circle or a pie chart. Divide it into 3 parts, in such a way that each part represents the relative size of WORK, REST, and FUN in your life. Here is an example:

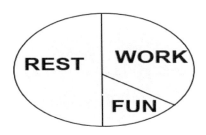

I leave it to you to decide what WORK, REST and FUN mean. Some people might include house chores in the FUN section. I guess most of us would probably include them under WORK.

What does the circle or chart say about your life? Is there room for change or do you have the balance right for your current circumstances?

Let's explore further: A quick and easy way to check is to rate the different aspects of your life. You can use a scale from 1 to 10, or simply use words such as Excellent, Very Good, Good, Neither Good or Bad, Needs Attention, In Really Bad Shape.

I suggest considering the following areas. Feel free to personalise this list:

- Social Connection
- Physical Activity
- Stress Management
- Attitude (think about gratitude, optimism, how you react to mistakes, etc.)

- Time-outs (me time, time out to recover, holidays)
- Variety
- Energy levels
- Giving back to society and contribution
- Your life purpose, that is to say, whether you have an idea of your purpose in life and it is easy for you to set priorities
- Nutrition
- Sleep
- Goals (how easy it is for you to set and follow them)
- Work satisfaction
- Any others?

Once you have a better idea of what your current balance situation looks like, summarise what your ideal balance in life would be like. What are the main challenges (or difficulties) that you are facing in bringing your life back into balance?

What areas of your life are working really well for you at the moment?

What words might other people use to describe you in relation to how balanced you are in your life?

What immediate changes can you introduce in order to make your life feel more balanced?

It's important to remember that life balance is an ongoing process and not just a means to an end. Life balance is much more than merely stating that you want something to happen, but is more about indicating the specifics of what you are GOING TO MAKE happen!

Unless you define the specific goals that you have for each of your main life areas, the chances of you actually achieving these goals will always be somewhat limited.

So, my final question for this section is, which of your main life areas are you going to bring back into balance first?

SELF-CARE TOOL #6: IF YOU FAIL TO PREPARE...

More at
The Companion

When you are feeling more or less all right, you could have a go at completing a table like the following as honestly as you can so that you can refer to it to get some help when you are not 100%.

(There is a completed example after the blank one.)

Take your time, as you will probably have some interesting insights while you think about it.

When I am well, I feel/think/do... this	Everyday activities that keep me well	Reminder list to keep me well

What would my family/friends notice if I were becoming unwell/emotionally depleted?	What do I want them to do?

When I am well, I feel/think/do... this	Everyday activities that keep me well	Reminder list to keep me well
1. I do not hide from feeling emotions. 2. I engage. 3. I am able to deal with my thoughts appropriately. 4. I can see the positive in a lot of things in addition to the negative. 5. I can give and receive.	1. I do not take unnecessary sick days. 2. I take time to take care of myself every day. 3. I have social interaction. 4. I read meaningful books. 5. I engage in meaningful work.	1. Believe in myself and follow my instincts. 2. Do not hide from emotions. 3. Stay in touch with people. 4. Be honest with/about my thoughts. 5. Enjoy banter.
What would my family/friends notice if I were becoming unwell/emotionally depleted?	What do I want them to do?	
1. They would know that I was taking unnecessary sick days. 2. They would notice I can't engage in banter. 3. They would notice their ideas/offers would be rejected. 4. They would notice I forget things. 5. They would notice mood swings. 6. They would notice I am tired/fatigued.	1. Listen to me compassionately. 2. Stay with me. 3. Invite me to go for a walk. 4. Be soft. 5. Reduce the amount of problems they share with me. 6. Express what they notice in me gently. 7. Check with me.	

Depending on your circumstances, you could prepare a similar table for your partner, so that they know SPECIFICALLY what to do when they see certain signs in you. It has to be very concrete and precise and you will need to adapt it to your partner's specific abilities. Examples might be essential. Maybe even photos of yourself demonstrating what you look like when you are tired, grumpy, running low on emotional fuel... If your partner has enough self-awareness, he/she may want to prepare his/her own table.

If you involve your partner, just be playful about it and remember he/she may not be as capable or enthusiastic about it as you are.

SELF-CARE TOOL #7: KNOW THY NEEDS

More at
The Companion Sometimes we don't know what we want, because we have lost touch with our needs.

A simple emotional needs audit can help identify imbalances in the way we are meeting our needs and areas for improvement.

It may draw attention to any unmet needs in your life and inspire some insights.

Here you will find a table that will allow you to carry out an audit of your emotions in a very simple way.

Just mark the rating that is closest to your experience (not at all, rarely, sometimes, often or always or most of the time).

Emotional needs	Not at all	Rarely	Sometimes	Often	Always or most of the time
Do you feel Safe and Secure in the main areas of your life?					
Do you feel there are people who need you? Do you get Attention from others?					
Do you have some Fun by engaging in hobbies, sports or activities with other people?					
Do you feel an Emotional connection to other people?					
Do you have Status or feel valued by others?					
Do you have time or space for Privacy when you need it?					
Do you feel you are Achieving something with your life?					
Do you feel in Control of the major areas of your life?					
Do you feel Engaged with life and that it is meaningful?					

You may have noticed some capital letters in the questions. They are there to help you identify different needs, such as the need for safety and security, etc.

Can you identify any specially unfulfilled need from your scores? Are they all more or less at the same level?

Can you think of ways to increase the scores of any particularly unfulfilled need? If so, are there any downsides to the change that is required? Does it seem too hard or time-consuming? Does it feel like another chore on your to-do list? Despite the downsides, do you think it is worth it? How will you feel when you have done it? Do you think it will benefit other people, too?

How do you feel while you are thinking of your own needs? Is it easy? Is it uncomfortable? Is there any pain?

If you find it really difficult to connect with your needs, that is all right. A question that sometimes helps is: If I had nothing to lose, if there were no restrictions whatsoever, if my actions didn't affect anybody else, what would I want to do right now? Finding an answer doesn't necessarily mean that it is desirable to go and do what we have discovered. It is a pointer in the direction of what we may really need.

It is important to know our needs well, not only so that we can do something in the direction of meeting them, but also because this knowledge can save us pain and uncomfortable situations later on.

Let's imagine that we are driving along a motorway. How would we know where our exit is if there were no visible signs and we had no GPS? In the same way, how would we know where our boundaries are if we didn't know what our needs are? Our needs are our responsibility.

A SHORT BONUS ON BOUNDARIES: Boundaries are expressions of our choices. They delineate where our responsibility ends and where somebody else's responsibility starts. Boundaries are never ways to control people.

It is very painful if we are only able to find where our boundaries are when we compromise them or when somebody violates them.

Being clear about our needs helps us set and express clear boundaries, which in turn saves us from painful breaches, resentment and/or anger later on.

Boundaries should be flexible enough to allow interconnection with other people, but at the same time, they should be strong enough to stop dangerous or detrimental things from entering. In that sense, we can think of boundaries by comparing them to the cell membranes of living organisms. Their semi-permeable structure lets nutrients in and at the same time keeps foreign bodies out.

The word "No" can be a powerful boundary, whether we use it to stop somebody hurting us or to stop ourselves from doing something harmful.

Do you have clear boundaries? If not, go back to the needs chart and see whether you could start choosing healthier boundaries in relation to each need.

Is it easy for you to communicate your boundaries calmly and clearly to others?

Do you find it easy to decide and express consequences for overstepping your boundaries?

Are you good at respecting other people's boundaries?

What are your boundaries like when it comes to stopping harmful things from affecting you?

What are your boundaries like when it comes to allowing supportive things into your life?

SELF-CARE TOOL #8:
THE PLACE WHERE
YOU SPEND MOST
OF YOUR TIME

If you take a look around the place where you spend most of your time (it may be your office, the kitchen, etc.), do you like what you see?

Is there clutter anywhere?

Is this place well-ventilated?

Could you bring more natural light in?

Could you make a little change today which would make the place feel more welcoming, peaceful, and joyful?

More at
The Companion   What would it need to transform it into your favourite place in the world? If you need inspiration, think in terms of your senses. Can you change or add something that looks, smells, feels, tastes, or sounds especially pleasant for you? For example, when you go into your space, ask yourself questions such as: What would really enhance it? What would I do if valued friends were coming round? Light a candle or incense? Clear things away? Put on some soft music?

We deserve to make it just as lovely for ourselves as we would for others.

A small step in that direction can act as a major mood boost!

By the way, have you got some space at home that you can call your own? A place where you can be undisturbed if you need to recharge your batteries or disconnect from your partner for a while? Have you decorated it with things that reflect your personality and your values?

Remember that objects hold energy, they can also remind us of people, our ideals, or our dreams. As Marie Condo says, pick them up and ask yourself "Does it spark love?" and decide whether you still want them in your space.

Chinese people believe that everything you display says something about you and attracts more of the same into your life. Does your space say what you want it to say about you and who you want to be? When you look at it, do you feel happy? Or are you still holding on to things from the past that don't reflect who you are now (old furniture, gifts you got that you don't really love, etc.)?

SELF-CARE TOOL #9: WHERE ATTENTION GOES, ENERGY FLOWS

A few years ago a friend told me to 'focus on the good' with regards to my marriage. I confess I didn't like hearing that because at that stage everything seemed to be going really badly.

However, it does help greatly to focus on the good, on the things I like about the relationship and the things I love and admire about my husband.

It is also a very healthy habit to look at the half of the glass that is full instead of the other half which is empty.

Psychologists have identified a fascinating element of human perception called cognitive dissonance (Festinger, L. (1957)). The main idea is that we cannot hold two opposing or contradictory impressions at the same time, so our minds need a criterion to decide really quickly which of the two contradictory impressions to believe.

How do our minds do that? They look for things that confirm them. If we already have certain memories, ideas or beliefs relating to one impression or the other, then we will unconsciously focus our attention only on those things that match or 'resonate' with those beliefs or thoughts, ignoring (filtering out) everything that would contradict and disprove them.

So basically, our brain tends to look for more of the same and to disregard new data that doesn't match what we already think. This is helpful in allowing us to maintain a consistent sense of self, but if we have suffered in our relationship, we may get into a vicious circle of expecting our partners to inflict more pain.

In order to train our mind so that it is not too difficult for us to look for the positives, when we go to bed at night, we can remember any pleasant moments we have had during the day. We can also keep a diary of positive experiences. If we do it every single day, we will notice that our mind focuses increasingly more on the positive things, ignoring the negative ones.

SELF-CARE TOOL #10: A LETTER OF SELF-APPRECIATION

Have you ever written a letter to yourself? As we explored in the previous self-care tool, the more we pay attention to the positive, the more our mind will focus on positive things automatically. Taking time to appreciate ourselves in writing will train our brains to focus on the positive qualities we have. Even if we are totally capable of recognising the positives in the world, we don't often see them in ourselves, so this tool can be surprisingly beneficial to extend that general capacity for appreciation to include ourselves, too.

You can be as creative as you want and play around with different ideas. Depending on your circumstances, it may be easy to start by writing a letter of appreciation to a younger version of yourself, perhaps at a time of your life when you felt really alive and bubbly.

Or perhaps you would prefer to write to a future self and appreciate the fact that he/she is taking more time to develop himself/herself and to be more genuine and happier.

Wherever you start, don't forget to write a letter of self-appreciation to yourself in the present as well.

Once you have chosen the version of yourself you are writing to, I would recommend handwriting the letter. If you are appreciating a really young version of yourself, perhaps you would like to experiment with writing with your non-dominant hand, the hand you would not use automatically for writing, as that would call for a slower pace and would usually produce a more child-like handwriting.

Express everything you appreciate about this version of yourself, focussing on strengths and ways of being rather than achievements and the things you do. For instance, if you are thinking about a time when your younger self did something selfless for somebody in need, instead of appreciating the behaviour so much, appreciate some aspects of your nature, such as empathy, generosity, courage, independent thinking, etc.

When you have finished writing, notice how you feel, put the letter in an envelope and ask somebody you trust to post it to you when you think you might need a reminder, on an especially difficult anniversary, a year later, etc.

Of course, you can do this as often as you want.

Getting a handwritten letter in the post is quite rare these days and it feels even more special if you have written it yourself and can't remember what you wrote.

If you cannot do it this way, perhaps you can schedule an email along these lines to be sent to you on a future date.

Or you can type your message on your computer or smartphone and set a reminder on your calendar to open the relevant file on a specific date in the future.

You can also experiment with enlisting a friend to post/hand you a little gift that you have got and wrapped up nicely for yourself in advance.

I find wrapping gifts really enjoyable and therapeutic. Do you?

SELF-CARE TOOL #11: OUR SPIRITUAL HOME

Have you got a regular practice that allows you to slow down and get in touch with your deepest truth?

Some people make gardening their spiritual home.

Others prefer a walk in nature.

For some people, their regular practice is sipping a cup of tea.

For others, it is praying, meditation or mindfulness.

Some people find their spiritual home when they are jogging and feeling fully alive.

Whatever it is, as long as it is not something detrimental to your health in any way, the key is regularity.

See if you can sustain practising it at more or less the same time and at more or less the same place.

You don't need anything special to return to your spiritual home. Just take a pause.

Find your own way to bring your attention inwards, acknowledge your thoughts, feelings, sensations, movements, and everything you experience.

Try to see them as mere products of your body-mind, and let all those experiences drop into the background of your awareness, while you just enjoy being alive.

If you are like me, you may find that you have different ways of returning home. I meditate, do some yoga, walk in nature, or go out in the garden.

SELF-CARE TOOL #12: FEEL THE CONNECTION

One of the things that make us the happiest is feeling connected to another person (from my experience, I would include pets here).

Perhaps a person on the spectrum would disagree and say that solitude or their special interest is what makes them the happiest, but right now, we are focusing on ourselves.

The best part of feeling connected is that quantity is not the main factor. It is the quality, the depth of the connection that really matters.

So it doesn't matter if it is a meaningful short exchange at the supermarket, on the phone or via email. What matters is that you are fully present, authentic, and open to noticing the connection, the things we have in common just because we are human beings.

Perhaps you will reach a point when you know that the other person has the same basic needs as you. They also need connection and make mistakes sometimes. They may be having a bad day. Your acknowledging their presence may change that for them... and for yourself.

I am not sure that this has been scientifically validated, but in my experience, if you are awake to feeling the connection with others, true moments of connection do happen.

It just takes a little attention, searching for opportunities to connect sincerely and deeply. It may be a small gesture of understanding, a wink, a kind word...

Connection is there already. We just need to express it... or acknowledge it when we are on the receiving end.

SELF-CARE TOOL #13: GRATITUDE

Research has found that being grateful increases positivity and happiness.

A good way of starting the day is investing a few moments in a few thoughts of appreciation and gratefulness. It need not be something big or contrived. We can be grateful for the warm bed we have (hopefully) woken up in, the roof over our heads, getting water on demand when we turn a tap, being able to do things (walk, see, hear...), our dear ones, the wonders of nature, kind gestures from others, etc. This is something I enjoy doing first thing in the morning, while I am still under the duvet.

For best results, again, it is important to turn gratitude into a regular practice. Try to incorporate it gradually into most of the things you experience. It is a very simple addition, but I can assure you it brings huge rewards.

SELF-CARE TOOL #14: PUTTING OUR THOUGHTS IN ORDER

Many times, when my granny used to ask my granddad what he was doing he would wink at me and say: 'I am putting my thoughts in order.' To this day, it continues to sound like a very wise answer to me!

Sometimes our mind is like a cluttered room. We get lots of thoughts and ideas but they may be confusing, illogical, dizzy-making. This is completely normal. When we are not focussing directly on something specific, our mind goes into default mode and generates lots of thoughts. It's like turning the radio to fill up space. And just like the radio, a lot of it will be just noise - not useful or particularly worth listening to.

It is useful to take some time off to clarify and put our thoughts in order.

An easy way of doing this is writing down as many thoughts as we can. Writing them down helps us define and prioritise thoughts, and it helps us declutter our mind, because we will most probably discover that some thoughts are just simply mental noise that is taking our attention away from what really matters to us.

I love a thought experiment I have heard from different sources. Let's imagine we are standing on the river bank, watching the river flow by. Sometimes, there is a leaf floating on the river. As we are watching it from the river bank, we have the option to follow the leaf with our gaze or to just continue watching the river. Perhaps another leaf will appear later. Our minds are a bit like the river. Every now and then we may perceive a thought, a feeling or a sensation. We can notice them and let them pass by or we can follow them until they disappear. This analogy helps me detach a bit from my thoughts and acknowledge that I am not my thoughts and in fact, I am more spacious than the thoughts.

The process of sorting and dumping our thoughts helps us experience who we really are, while we are still aware of any passing thoughts.

Once we feel we have finished sorting and dumping, it is great to do something that soothes us before plunging back into activity.

When we do this kind of process, we usually find something like empty clear space, so it is important to be mindful and refrain from embarking immediately on hectic or stressful activity or else that precious empty space and neater mind will soon be filled up with junk thoughts again.

You can't please everybody; you are not chocolate!

SELF-CARE TOOL #15: FUN FOOD

I know that food is a very sensitive topic for most of us. Food has so many meanings, but especially for us, food can mean comfort, it may become some sort of compensation for the emotional reciprocity we so crave for in our relationship.

So it is often useful to start taking a gentle, yet honest, look at our relationship with food. We may notice interesting patterns, such as the fact that we may either be following somebody else's habit ('Mum loved to eat...') or rebelling against it ('At home, if we didn't eat up the main meal, we were not allowed to have any dessert, so I will now indulge in....').

Perhaps, you may notice that you are adapting so much to your partner's limited range of allowed foods that you rebel when you go out for a meal without him/her.

In my opinion, the main point about eating is the atmosphere in which you eat. Can you be relaxed for a few moments in order to savour and enjoy the meal? Can you consider meal-time 'me-time', a time to reconnect with your needs and your body? Can you perhaps even shift your attention a little to what the food does for you? Can you have a moment of appreciation for all those people who have made it possible for you to have the ingredients or the meal today?

When I was little we would occasionally say a prayer before meals, but that was not the norm. As a young adult I learned a short Sanskrit text by heart and now I say it before each meal.

I say it aloud if I am with my husband or just mentally if I feel other people won't appreciate it. It is a way of relaxing the mind and body, as well as a way of appreciating the intelligence and energy that the food contains, which will be incorporated into my body.

For many of us, meal times may be lonely times. When our partners are anxious, they may not be able to cope with the way we chew or our table manners and we may end up eating alone. We went through that for about a month, when my husband was under a lot of stress. He just snapped and told me 'You are revolting. I will not eat with you ever again.' It is a very painful experience, especially if we come from a family where mealtimes were the time to catch up and connect.

If mealtimes are difficult for you, accept your feelings around the situation, talk about it in your support group. In my own experience, it worked wonders to hear somebody say that they had gone through exactly the same experience. This feeling of common humanity, that I was not the only one in the huge universe going through this, lifted the pain immediately. It may sound weird, but that has been my experience. Not feeling alone had a strong, immediate therapeutic effect for me, and many others have commented on similar positive effects of feeling that other people are going through the same thing.

Back to the topic of food, if your partner has food sensitivities and idiosyncrasies, make sure to retain some of the foods that match your identity in your diet, even if it means having something different from what your partner is having. We tend to morph into the person that our partner needs. The gain from this simple act that reminds you of the importance of retaining your identity may be worth the extra effort in meal planning and preparation.

Can you make cooking and your meals as much fun as possible? Does your food appeal to all your senses? If fun means adding more spices to your own food, then why not? If fun means moulding your food into different shapes... if fun means having an array of textures, colours, and tastes on your plate, just allow yourself to have fun.

A variety of tastes in the same meal will keep you satisfied for much longer than if you only have say, only salty or sweet dishes.

There is a very strong correlation between our food and our mood. Make the most of it by eating healthy food that gives you joy!

I don't know about you, but in my case, my mood in the early morning sets the mood for the rest of the day, so I am going to share a quick, fun breakfast (you might say it is a bit childish. My inner child doesn't mind and I know that I can't make everybody happy). It is called Date and Almond Hearts. You need very few ingredients.

Here is my way of making them: I boil or steam some dry dates (without the stones) and I blanch some almonds. I grind the almonds coarsely with some seeds. Sunflower seeds go really well. If I boil the dates, they may still have some water when they are ready, so I keep the water, which is golden brown and sweet, aside for decoration. I puree the dates with a fork and add some vanilla essence. I add the almond/seed mix, some grated coconut or creamed coconut, and some raw cacao.

Then I mix everything well and mould it with the help of a cookie cutter (I have some heart-shaped ones). I decorate around the heart with the 'syrup' that I have saved from cooking the dates. This is something simple, so my husband enjoys it too! The variant on the photo has a smaller heart on top, made with walnuts and blueberries.

Yesterday I learned how to make plant-based buttermilk: add 1 tablespoon of apple cider vinegar or lemon juice to 2 cups of plant-based milk (the higher the protein content, the better, so they suggested using soya or hemp milk). Set it aside while you prepare the rest of the ingredients for your recipe. Buttermilk gives your batter a fluffier texture. I can't wait to try it in vegetarian pancakes, maybe even the next time I bake scones.

Get your creative juices flowing and have fun in the kitchen!

More at
The Companion

◆ ◆ ◆

SELF-CARE TOOL #16: UPLIFTING SMELLS

DID YOU KNOW?

The area of the brain that processes information relating to the sense of smell is in very close proximity to a part of the brain that processes emotional information

Some smells bring memories of comfort (like baking smells, the fragrance of freshly-made coffee, vanilla essence, your favourite flower or freshly cut grass) and they may give you an instant mood boost.

Do you know why aroma scents are related to emotions?

Because the aroma centres in the brain are in close proximity to the mood centres, they take a direct route to the limbic system (which governs emotion and memory).

Citrus aromas help lift your mood and have anti-stress properties. Even smelling some freshly cut lemon fruit will do. If you prefer, you can smell or use some citrus essential oil, such as lemon, orange or neroli.

Frankincense and spearmint are uplifting oils which also help your attention and focus.

If you are new to essential oils, please notice that you can use them on an aroma diffuser or in the water for your bath. They are generally too strong to be applied neat on your skin.

You can dilute them in a carrier (like almond or jojoba oil) and apply a few drops on your wrists. You can also put a few drops in a handkerchief or tissue and keep it with you.

The best time to use uplifting oils is in the morning, or any time before 6pm. After that, it would be better to use more calming aromas, such as lavender or chamomile.

SELF-CARE TOOL #17: REST MATTERS

Isn't life wonderful when we are rested? Well, having a regular daily routine helps us establish a healthy waking/sleep pattern. Most people need around 8 hours of sleep at night. Some may be OK with a bit more or a bit less.

If we (or our partners) work shifts or during the night, it is especially important for us to have at least some sleep at the same time every night. For instance, we may sleep from 10pm to 6am most days, and when we work shifts, we may sleep from 3am to 11am, in which case we would always be sleeping consistently between 3am and 6am.

The night time offers our minds and bodies a chance to metabolise the nutrients and experiences we have incorporated during the day, extracting what we need and disposing of the unwanted materials and memories.

Make the most of the time before going to bed. If you can, have a routine that will allow you to wind down gradually, reducing screen time, listening to calming music, visualising that you are putting your experiences and emotions from the day away in an imaginary box, adopting an attitude of gratitude for the day, and inviting your mind to become quieter and get ready for some restorative sleep. This is a great time to write down any thoughts. Downloading them to paper can help you to put them aside for the night.

A little self massage before bedtime can help with mild sleeping problems, especially if you massage your feet. You can use a bit of oil or body lotion.

A friend suggested visualising that as we undress, we are also letting go of all the experiences from our day. This is especially helpful if we have had a particularly stressful or painful day. We can have the intention to remove the tension and pain at the same time we take off our clothes.

SELF-CARE TOOL #18: MUSIC

Music helps us to connect with our emotions and also to reach a more regulated state.

We may just sit and listen to our favourite music, play some uplifting music and sing along, or play some upbeat music and dance along. We may also do some percussion work (it is really great for emotions). If we haven't got a drum, we can tap on a table or desk.

 You can create your own playlists with different kinds of music.

My favourite music for singing is:

Brave by Sarah Bareilles

Titanium by Sia

Firework by Katy Perry

Yellow by Coldplay (Don't ask me why. I can't resist it.)

My favourite songs for dancing or exercising are:

I'm in love with your body by Ed Sheeran

What makes you beautiful by One Direction

Uptown Funk by Mark Robson

Despacito by Luis Fonsi

Music that is always uplifting for me:

Time to wander and *A Perfect 2* by Gypsy and The Cat

Brave by Sarah Bareilles

Which are yours?

SELF-CARE TOOL #19: INTENTIONAL LIVING

I know it may be difficult for some of us to think about our life purpose.

It seems too vast, too important or elusive sometimes.

So let's try to break it down into more manageable pieces: how about thinking about the things that make you feel alive, the little things you enjoy?

For instance, if you enjoy gardening, next time you are tending to the plants and soil, notice what you appreciate so much about it. Is it the generosity of life, which multiplies those little seeds you sow into beautiful plants and perhaps many flowers and fruits?

Perhaps you like noticing that a little bird is watching you.

Perhaps you feel connected with nature, with something bigger than yourself, that was there before you and will continue to be there after you; something you can rely on.

Perhaps you like finding little stones and feeling their strength, noticing the stubbornness of some weeds that keep cropping up no matter what you do...

During moments like these, you may feel that your life purpose is just being there to bear witness and appreciate all this, and I would agree.

I think our life purpose is not necessarily about carving

ourselves a space in the history of mankind, but doing what we are doing with focussed attention and a positive intention, no matter how mundane or insignificant it may seem.

I also think that our life purpose can change in time,

It is what makes life worth living.

As Viktor E. Frankel wrote in Man's Search for Meaning (Frankel, 2004) 'A man who becomes conscious of the responsibility he bears toward a human being who affectionately waits for him, or to an unfinished work, will never be able to throw away his life. He knows the "why" for his existence, and will be able to bear almost any "how".'

So, what is your life purpose right now?

More at
The Companion

SELF-CARE TOOL #20: T-SHIRT SLOGANS

When I am struggling with a difficult experience (such as a challenging situation, thought or emotion), I find that encapsulating the experience or my wish about it into a slogan on a T-shirt is a fun way of getting some distance between me and the experience. It helps me gain some objectivity, especially if I am feeling stuck. This is something that always makes me laugh.

Here are some of my own examples:

WARNING: It might not be a good idea to wear the following T-shirt when your autistic partner is around. The word 'no' doesn't seem to work with many autistic people (more on this on Part Two: EXPLORATION #24). In my husband's case, I think NO means 'keep insisting until she changes that to a YES', so when I mean NO, I have learned to transform it into coming up with a couple of alternatives (only 2, OK? otherwise he may get too confused). In that way, he can choose another option that I can say YES to.

I can get really absorbed in trying different colours, drawings; getting the text more or less right... It is quite therapeutic for me. There are plenty of online sites where you can have a go at it if

More at
The Companion

you feel inspired to try.

❖ ❖ ❖

SELF-CARE TOOL #21: MAY OUR VOICES BE HEARD

My playing small doesn't serve life

It is very common in NT-ASD relationships to have our voices muted. We can't always express everything we want to express, or we may need to tailor the way we communicate things so that we can have a chance of getting them across to our partners.

One of the factors that may contribute to us not saying what we want to say is related to **Affective Deprivation Disorder.** Basically, we start acting as if there is no point in communicating because we don't feel truly understood, seen, heard, or paid attention to.

Sometimes you will see that people use another name, **Ongoing Traumatic Relationship Syndrome**, to describe what some of us experience in these kinds of relationships. The reference to ongoing trauma reflects the fact that normally there is not one major traumatic event (such as the trauma people experience during a war) but rather a series of repeated smaller traumatic incidents, which many people outside the relationship wouldn't notice.

Sometimes, the effects of our kind of relationships receive the name of **Cassandra Syndrome** or **Cassandra Phenomenon**.

I think the name Cassandra Syndrome is very revealing. In Greek mythology, the god Apollo granted Cassandra the gift of foreseeing the future in order to seduce her. When she rejected him, Apollo cursed her so that even though she still had the gift to see what would happen, nobody would believe her.

You may have already heard about Cassandra Syndrome. I really resonate with the experience of knowing something and not being believed. If you also resonate with it, pause and think about when it started in your life. Was it present from the beginning of your relationship with your partner? (perhaps even before if there were instances of autism in your family of origin). Do you think it developed gradually over time for you?

How many times in your relationship or due to it, have you felt that people didn't believe you? Have you ever talked to people who know your partner about aspects of your life at home only for them to deny your reality saying that your partner is not like that at all?

Different people describe Cassandra Syndrome in different ways. I see this Cassandra effect playing in two ways in my life: the first one involves my husband and the second one involves people outside our relationship.

Let's look at the first one. I think that, although it has improved in the past few years, my husband's emotional self-awareness is not his greatest strength. It is sometimes difficult for him to identify and express what he is feeling. I can see micro-changes in his body language, tone of voice, etc. and I sometimes share what I see if I think it might help him identify it, but more often than not, that doesn't end well. Sometimes he even blames me as if I had the power to create that feeling in him by bringing it to his awareness. It is a very painful situation to be in.

It is like seeing there is going to be a "train wreck" and not being able to stop it. I see it in painful detail and I also see the aftermath, but no matter what I say, my partner won't believe me.

I would like to share with you specific details of how this manifests in our marriage. I will be sharing very personal experiences in the hope that you will gain some insights if you experience something similar. It is not an easy topic for me to reflect upon, let alone with somebody else, but I wish I had known about this long ago and it is my hope to spare you some unnecessary suffering if you are going through something remotely similar.

Autistic traits usually lead to *faux pas*, some social blunders that sometimes people find hilarious or unacceptable, and we (the partners) may find embarrassing and painful, especially if we don't know that our partner is not doing it on purpose because we are not aware of autism yet. In our relationship, this tends to happen when my husband wants to become friends with a lady. He doesn't know how to assess whether his attention is welcome or not. When it comes to interpersonal relationships, he seems to have two settings: ALL and NOTHING. So when he wants to establish a friendship with a lady, he tends to go all in. By that I mean that he will hyper-focus on what the lady needs. He will help her in any way he can imagine, he will spend many hours talking to her, thinking about her, talking to me about her, doing things for her, buying her birthday presents, emailing her or writing her notes, and basically giving her a lot of time, energy and attention. Unfortunately, the Cassandra in me sees all that from the initial stages and I am damned if I do and damned if I don't with regards to mentioning what I see. I want to remind my husband that:

- people have boundaries;
- we have different degrees of connection with people, and some behaviours are only reserved to those who are close to us;
- friendships take time to develop and we should be open but cautious;
- he should check with the other person to see that they are not getting the wrong idea (i.e. that they believe there is something romantic or sexual involved);
- etc. etc.

I have tried many different strategies. I have drawn concentric circles which represent an increasingly distant connection, putting my husband's name in the centre and placing me and his family close and everybody else where we thought they belonged (this is a bit what you would do for your child, isn't it?). I have talked to him about trust and boundaries. Have you done that, too? I have also looked the other way. None of these methods have worked. He is clueless. He denies. He explains that his intentions are innocent. He gets furious at me for interfering. He gets confused. He sends mixed messages to all involved. He behaves as if he is obsessed with her. He sometimes even tells the other lady that she is his obsession. And then, the lady in question turns against him.

This pattern has already played out a few times in our marriage over the years. It has not happened after his diagnosis, so I am hoping the assessment has brought an unexpected bonus of social awareness. I am not the same person, either. I have done my work and I also know which therapist to turn to before things get too messy.

Mind you, I now know that my husband's intentions are good. In most cases, he is trying to help the lady in distress because she is having difficulties at work or relationship problems of her own.

So, as you can imagine, he loves the feeling of being her knight in shining armour. Besides, her problems are not his fault at all so he doesn't need to do anything about them, and this attempt at friendship blocks his anxiety and other personal problems out of his thinking mind. I can see how seductive the whole thing can be for my husband! No wonder his mind gets so caught in this!

Now, I think we owe Apollo another unspoken curse. (Brace yourself, this is my own personal theory.) Among other things, Apollo is the god of truth. As you probably know, another typical autistic trait is valuing truth more than feelings, which in this case, means that he has no problem whatsoever sharing with me details of things that have happened or what he likes with regards to the other lady. At the same time, he is totally clueless of how invisible, unheard, confused, self-doubting, ignored, frustrated, and furious I feel in situations like these. (By the way, I know the reaction to my husband's actions is all mine and I do what I can to work on it.)

The second way in which Cassandra syndrome manifests in my life occurs when I dare to share what life is like at home outside the group of people who really get it (mostly because they have had first hand experience). This was even worse before his autism was discovered and assessed. My words were met with disbelief. People who knew my husband pitied him for being married to this mad, bossy woman! Mad and bossy I may be, but I know my husband!

At least, after his official assessment, I had a report to prove that what I had seen and was speaking about was true and not my imagination.

Still to this day, some people who know my husband and know about autism comment he is so empathic and always willing to help. Sometimes I do explain that my husband has a huge heart and he can certainly be empathic and willing to help but the effort of doing so is so huge that when he gets back home he is exhausted, needs time alone to recover, and is not available for anything or anybody else (i.e. me). Sometimes I just keep quiet and smile because I don't think outsiders will understand no matter what I say and they will (once again) think I am a mad, bossy hag.

So I need to be able to speak about my reality in environments that won't question my sanity, but resonate, validate, and understand. I think it is imperative to meet this need regularly in a safe environment. If you haven't got a space like this in your life yet, please start researching support groups, specialist therapists, online forums, etc. There is a list of resources at the end of this book to get you started. If you did some research a few years ago and didn't find the right support, please consider researching again. There is much more available now.

Have you got regular opportunities to have reciprocal interactions with other people in which you are free to express whatever you want without it being turned against you?

Have you also got opportunities to allow your voice to be heard on a regular basis outside circles related to autism, too? It may be within your local community or a religious group, or campaigning for a cause you consider worthwhile, for example.

Besides, have you got regular opportunities for expressing disagreement in healthy ways, to experience that it is OK to disagree and that disagreements don't necessarily always lead to arguments or meltdowns?

This is a relational matter, so if your circumstances don't allow you to talk to somebody else, talk to yourself. You can talk to your image in a mirror or on a video conferencing app or you can even talk to the portrait of somebody you trust and respect if there is no other option. Remember that this is not something that starts and finishes in yourself, but it is the effect of what happens when you communicate your reality to others and they just don't get it, so it is important to see a reassuring face looking back at you while you are talking.

If you prefer, you can talk to your pet, as long as it is the kind of pet which can pay attention to you. I don't think that talking to a goldfish will have the healing effect we are after.

I would like to invite you to journal on how this may be affecting you. It is not uncommon to experience anger or rage because of all the things we have bottled up inside when we felt nobody could see what we saw.

When I feel like I am about to explode with anger (or sometimes afterwards), I check whether there is something I keep saying that falls into deaf ears and I look for ways to release the emotion safely, while acknowledging that everybody is allowed to have their own experience. It is like what my husband and I learned a while ago: if you draw a big number 6 on a sheet of paper and put it between 2 people, one will see a 6 all right, but the other will see a 9. They are both right from their different points of view, aren't they?

SELF-CARE TOOL #22: STEPPING OUT OF OUR NORMAL ROLES

I can't suffer enough to make anyone's life better

During a normal day, we usually play different roles. Some of those roles may be related to our work, our family, our social status, or our duties at home.

However, our mental wellbeing can get compromised if we stick to some of those roles so much that we identify with them. We can't expect (or be expected) to be "the dutiful partner", "the loving parent", and "the efficient worker" (to give some examples of what I mean by roles) all the time. It is healthy to have opportunities to step out of our usual roles.

I have read something that I find very enlightening and

inspiring about this in a book. The context here is getting identified with the role of the helper or the helped.

> *'When we are able to step outside our situations for a moment and recognize the constrictions, we may even be prepared to acknowledge that somehow we ourselves are contributing to this sense of imprisonment.*
>
> *There's great potential in that recognition alone. It's the beginning of our escape. Just to be alert to the entrapment can prevent it from taking complete hold without our conscious awareness. We're more on the lookout for ways to penetrate the walls: a loose brick here, a vent duct there. We find an opportunity and grasp it and suddenly begin to come out from behind the roles.'*
>
> (Dass and Gorman, 2001)

When we are performing our roles all the time, we can struggle to truly connect with other people and we can lose touch with the vulnerable side of our humanity.

So as Ram Dass and Paul Gorman suggest, we need to start by recognising the fact that we got trapped in one or several roles.

More at
The Companion Let's then list the main roles we currently perform in our lives in any order. (You will find some samples below, but it is important that each of us identifies our own. So after reading this section, perhaps you will want to turn to the relevant section on the Companion resource).

Some usual roles

Cassandra;
the pet-lover;
the good friend;
the parent;
the dutiful partner;
the untiring housekeeper;
the doting relative;
the lover of beauty;
the hard-working bread-winner;
the long-suffering person;
the rescuer;
the hero(ine);
the servant;
the victim;
the child;
the responsible adult;
the healer;
the warrior;
the cheerleader;
the wizard;
the jester;
the innocent;
the ruler;
the regular girl/guy;
the lover;
the caregiver;
the explorer;
the sage;
the entertainer;
the host(ess);
the expert;
the creator;
the destroyer;
the sustainer; ...

Next, go over your list and see whether there is at least a dominant role. How easy is it for you to take "holidays" from that role? How do you feel when you do that? Do you sense any guilt, perhaps because you fear disappointing somebody in particular? Just notice without any judgement.

Do you feel the level of "devotion" to your roles is healthy for you and for all those involved? If not, what baby step could you take in the next few days to break the identification with that role?

We also need opportunities to step out of our normal caring partner/personal assistant roles. It is very easy to get into parent-child roles in our relationships, especially if we were parentified in our childhood, that is to say, if the circumstances in our family of origin were such that we had to assume adult responsibilities at a tender age. This may be due to having many younger siblings to look after or due to ill-health in one or both of our parents, for instance.

If it is easy or natural for you to slip into a role that involves taking over your partner's tasks or responsibilities, a healthier role would be that of a mentor for your partner. A mentor shows how things are done, helps when help is requested or offers help (and accepts that not all offers of help will be welcome), but doesn't take over the mentee's responsibilities or activities.

Moreover, due to the nature of our relationships, there is not much reciprocity or shared responsibility and we may end up allowing our partners to make all the decisions while we take all the responsibility.

If jumping in to help is indeed one of your patterns of behaviour, then consider the possibility of having a brief, to the point, scheduled chat with your partner (go to Part 2 of the book if you want more on communication) and check whether they trust you enough to come and ask for help if they are confused by something or in a difficult situation. Check whether they feel comfortable when you ask them for help. Check whether they feel comfortable if you offer your help. In my "wise moments", I ask him "Is there anything I can do to help?" Even when my husband might not be able to articulate what he would like me to do at that moment, an open question like this gives him a chance to express what is going on for him. He may have a confused look on his face, but perhaps he is just thinking hard.

If lack of reciprocity or shared responsibility plays in our relationships, we may allow our partners to dictate how we should do things while we may feel powerless and comply because we find meltdowns or put downs too high a toll to pay.

In relationships with a person on the autism spectrum, there may be a lot of unilateral financial control, so it is good to have opportunities for us to spend some money in a way we choose.

We may experience a lot of inflexibility, so it is crucial to have opportunities to change our plans without negative consequences, to be playful, and to feel free in our soul.

Just check what your usual dynamic might be right now... and step out of it by assuming a totally different role when you are alone or with other people in order to keep balance in your life and to regain self-confidence.

SELF-CARE TOOL #23:
ONE STEP AT A TIME

When we are in stressful situations, difficult thoughts and emotions pull us away from the kind of person we would like to be and the people and things we care about.

When I feel some disconnect or that something is not right and I don't know what is going on, I ask myself "What do I want/need?"

Sometimes I get an answer that in itself reveals where the trigger or issue may be, but there are also times I just can't find the answer no matter what I do.

I have found a trick that makes it easier for me. I ask myself "What is ONE STEP I can take to feel a bit better right now?"

I usually get an answer to that. Maybe "Oh, well, I can go out in the garden." Or "I can move that clutter out of the way." Or even "I can sit on the couch and have a cup of herbal tea."

Reflecting about the kind of person I want to be right now also helps me.

If you prefer, you can think about somebody you admire and focus on the values they represent. If you value that person's strength, how can you orient your next step towards feeling a bit stronger? If you value that person's courage, what would be a courageous next step for you?

What helps you take one step towards feeling a bit better?

Once you start feeling a bit better, you will naturally reconnect with your deepest goals for your life and you will gain a wider perspective of where you are and what the next step may be.

SELF-CARE TOOL #24:
SMILING ON DEMAND

When we smile deliberately, even if there is no other reason for smiling than wanting to feel better, "happy hormones" get produced, which boost our mood.

If you are in a situation where smiling would be inappropriate, try to imagine an inner smile.

Get playful! You can try different kinds of smiles; you can try to imagine smiling with different parts of your body, you can impersonate different people or characters.

The other day I was really angry. I remembered to smile and there happened to be a mirror where I was. I looked in the mirror and the image didn't really look like a smile, more like a sinister grin I would say, but it did the trick anyway! It made me laugh and changed my mental chip.

Changing your body language or posture can also help you change your state. For example, taking up more space with your body (striking a power/superhero pose, creating a snow angel on the ground, or doing an expansive yoga pose) can have a beneficial effect on your mind.

SELF-CARE TOOL #25: SABOTAGING YOUR SABOTEUR

Sometimes there is an inner part of ourselves which, surely with the very best of intentions, stops us from doing what we feel is the right thing to do.

Sometimes that part is very concerned about the effects a different action would have on our dear ones. We are afraid of rocking the boat because we may fear they will criticise us or disapprove of us.

Sometimes, we abort our attempts because we are afraid of making mistakes. We may have gone through painful experiences when we made a mistake in the past and we were humiliated or punished for it.

Sometimes we may feel exhausted, but instead of resting we may go for a cup of coffee or some chocolate to pick us up so that we can carry on giving, for instance.

Can you find the main reason why you sabotage your attempts?

Can you catch your saboteur red-handed?

Can you get to know your saboteur and its *modus operandi*? How does your saboteur seduce/force you to follow his/her guidance?

Does your saboteur speak in a familiar voice, in the voice of somebody you know?

I suggest giving your saboteur a descriptive name, such as "The Temptress" or "The Bully". Next time he/she wants to take over, offer them gratitude for trying to be helpful, but reassure them that you have a more important task for them. Let's see what this might be like through a more concrete example. In the previous scenario in which you are feeling exhausted, The Temptress may start reminding you of that velvety bar of chocolate so and so has given you, where it is, how much you want it, and how good you will feel after having a bit, only a bit... if you can stop eating it, because it is really, really good and you really, really deserve it after all that work/study/stress/exercise/loneliness... You can tell The Temptress: "I can see you and I am impressed by your fantastic memory, attention to detail, and good intention. Thank you. I know where that chocolate is. Could you help me with a more vital job, which is to remind me to stop and drink some sips of water when I start feeling exhausted? I think part of the tiredness may be a sign of dehydration. If that doesn't work, would you remind me to take a little rest?"

Practice (persistence) usually does the trick.

SELF-CARE TOOL #26: THE OPTIMUM LEVEL OF PERFORMANCE

More at
The Companion Think about what happens when you are under stress. Does your level of performance change? That is to say, do you tend to undertake even more things than usual or do you just collapse and find it difficult to do anything?

Some of us have a tendency to over-perform when under stress: we start committing to more, we push ourselves more, we speed up, etc. Some of us have a tendency to under-perform when under pressure or stress: we start procrastinating, we become slower, and we act as if we don't really care.

It is really interesting to watch ourselves and discover whether we can keep our optimum level of performance and commitment even when we are under pressure or whether we tend to over- or under-perform.

Are we happy taking everybody else's share of responsibility and do we feel resentful and depleted afterwards? If we underperform, do we end up with a backlog of things to do or perhaps a guilty conscience?

Have you ever stopped to investigate which your main pattern is when you are under pressure?

Once you have worked out the main performance style you

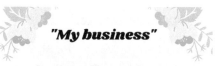

"Not my circus"

what other people perceive or believe

what others think of me

adopt when you are stressed, if you are not happy with it, reflect about what you can do to bring it closer to its optimum level.

Here are some suggestions for the **over-performers**:

Can you shift your attention to any real responsibility you may be neglecting? (e.g. your health, your relationship, your self-esteem, etc.).

Can you refrain from taking on tasks or problems which are not your responsibility? (I once read the sentence "It is not my circus, they are not my monkeys". If I bring it to mind, it is useful because it makes me laugh).

Can you tolerate the discomfort that others may feel without taking it on so that they can deal with their own problems?

And here are some suggestions for the **under-performers**:

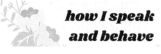

"My business"

what and who I give time, energy and attention to

my response to other people's behaviour

the boundaries I set

what, who and when to forgive

how I speak and behave

Can you think of any long-term benefits to stopping delaying doing something that you need to do?

If somebody volunteers to take over, can you be assertive and say that you are willing to do it yourself? Can you then follow it through?

If you under-perform because you start having negative thoughts about yourself when under pressure (e.g. around being inadequate, about not having enough qualifications, around not being strong enough, etc.), can you find 3 examples to contradict those negative thoughts from past successes in your life?

SELF-CARE TOOL #27: STEPPING INTO NATURE

You may have experienced moments when you see a picture of a place of natural beauty and you get absorbed in it.

You may experience a feeling of expansion, of slowing down, of calming down, perhaps even the recognition of connection with nature, or the feeling that you belong here.

Is there any way in which you can connect with nature right now? Could you go to a park, a hill, or a riverbank and take a stroll there? Could you step into your garden? If it is safe, would you walk barefoot? Or perhaps, could you tend to your indoor plants or even hold some seashells or pebbles in your hands while you admire their perfection just the way they are?

Every act of connecting with nature, no matter how simple or small it may seem, may be just what you need to reconnect with curiosity, awe, joy or other positive emotions.

SELF-CARE TOOL #28: CLOSURE

Moments of disconnect happen in all relationships. Then one of the partners may apologise and the couple will make up. There is closure.

The nature of our relationships may make it more difficult for us to find closure.

We don't usually get such a luxury in our relationship. There may be an upsetting experience, we may want to clear the air, we may want to do what we can to make it right, but our partners are not interested. They may have already forgotten about it, they may have seen the situation in a totally different light and can't see the point of talking about it (they know they are right and we are wrong. Why talk about it?).

We are left with an open wound.

There are simple steps you can take to tend to that wound:

You can journal about it: you can write about it or, if writing is not your thing, you can try recording yourself on audio or even video.

By the way, have you ever tried recording yourself when you are really angry or upset? Listening to your "rant" will bring new realisations. You will notice how you emphasise certain words, the emotions your voice conveys, your pauses, the ease or resistance you feel towards getting close to the real issue. If you can record yourself on video, you will certainly notice your body language and gestures. One day I was recording a video at home for a presentation and things were not going well at all. My husband had shown keen interest in being behind the camera, but on the day of the recording, he seemed absolutely clueless. (Since then, among other things, I have learned that the fact that autistic people were able to do one thing yesterday doesn't guarantee they will be able to do it again today). The clock was ticking and we were not getting anywhere. I was very nervous and got furious at him. At one point, he left the camera rolling and I didn't notice it. When I watched the video later on, I was shocked! When I was aware that the camera was on and delivering the presentation, I was all smiles, confident, and kind. When things went wrong and I thought my husband had stopped recording, I immediately turned into a raging monster. I just couldn't believe the way I was shouting at my husband that day. I was not using abusive language or being physically abusive. What shocked me was my face, the exasperated tone of voice, the way I said his name... it seemed to convey disgust. It was a huge lesson for me.

Just make sure your journaling or your audio/video material is totally secure and that nobody else will have access to it, so that you can feel comfortable expressing fully and freely.

Another option is to look for a song whose mood resonates with the wound. Listen to it and let your emotions flow. You may want to dance or move to it. Looking for the right song will help you identify what you feel. Then, if you let the emotion move your body, as Taylor Swift's song suggests, it may help you "Shake it off".

You may want to speak to somebody you trust, who will be able to be there for you without judging either you or your partner.

SELF-CARE TOOL #29: PLAN AN ENJOYABLE EVENT

You may be pleasantly surprised to know that the mere fact of planning an enjoyable event gives us an emotional boost.

We are looking forward to it, we count the days to get there, and we have additional motivation for our daily activities.

Once that event has taken place, plan another one.

Having a pleasant event to look forward to makes us feel more alive.

SELF-CARE TOOL #30: TURN TO YOUR LOCAL COMMUNITY

Getting involved in a community cause that matters to you will help widen your horizons, connect with people, and find new meaning.

If you don't know of any such causes in your area and you are in the UK, you may want to check out the following websites:

https://doit.life/volunteer

https://www.ncvo.org.uk/ncvo-volunteering/i-want-to-volunteer

https://www.volunteerscotland.net/

https://volunteering-wales.net/

https://www.sportandrecreation.org.uk/pages/volunteering/

https://mycauseuk.com/

❖ ❖ ❖

SELF-CARE TOOL #31: REWARDS, PLEASE

In order to make it easier for you to incorporate self-care *consistently* in your life, you may consider rewarding yourself for each act of self-care you perform.

Some of us might want to make it a double-whammy by using money as an immediate reward and then using the money as savings for another, bigger, reward. For instance, we may have a jar and put a coin there for every 3 self-care activities we undertake.

Other kinds of reward may be more social in nature, like shopping with a fun friend or inviting friends for tea.

Some rewards may involve an edible treat, a warm drink or time to read a book, to watch a film, to do some knitting or any activity which we really enjoy (dancing/singing/painting, maybe?), which are also self-care activities so you can reward yourself again!

SELF-CARE TOOL #32: ME & TIME

We never seem to have enough time for all the things we need or want to do. Or perhaps we have so much time on our hands that we are bored and without motivation to do anything. Is there anything you can do to get your schedule into a better shape?

You can, for instance, use a very simple yet effective time management matrix like the one by Dwight D. Eisenhower, (yes, the man who was US president in the 50s). His basic idea was very simple, really:

The priority we should assign to a task is related both to its importance and its urgency. The higher the priority, the more attention and time it deserves.

Steven Covey, author of *The Seven Habits of Highly Effective People,* has developed this idea further into a model with four quadrants. You can represent his concept on a very simple table, like the one that follows, and complete the relevant fields.

Although this is a very simple activity, it can give you profound insight into what you value most in life.

More at
The Companion   You may want to complete your own chart at The Companion.

	URGENT	NOT URGENT
IMPORTANT	Here go the things that are really necessary. TOP PRIORITY	Here are the things that are often critical to our own values but get little time (such as rest, fun, connection, health)
NOT IMPORTANT	These are often other people's agendas and not our own (for instance, an email that arrives needing urgent attention or phone calls). Moderation is advised.	These are things we use to distract ourselves, such as watching TV or YouTube/cleaning our sock drawer, etc. Reduce them as much as you can.

For instance, I once completed this table and the result looked like the version you will see below...

	URGENT	NOT URGENT
IMPORTANT	*Housework. Gainful employment. Being a good wife/sister/ neighbour/worker.*	*My medical/dental appointments. Sleeping 8 hours a day. Holidays and fun time! Watching informative, fun, or uplifting YouTube videos.*
NOT IMPORTANT	*Doing everything everybody asks for right away. Replying to all messages and emails as soon as I get them.*	*Watching silly YouTube videos just to kill time. Keeping up with the latest gossip.*

If your table looks like that, it may be time to go back to *SELF-CARE TOOL #3: FROM INTENTIONS TO ACTION.*

Once you have a version of the table that reflects your current experience truthfully, ask yourself: does it match your values?

For instance, I really value connection! When I notice that connection has ended up in the "Not important/Not urgent" quadrant, I don't need to look any further for explanations for why I am feeling so cranky and depleted! I need to do something about it, which usually involves doing something that reflects the fact that it is now in the "Important/Urgent" quadrant. At times, I may place it in the "Important/Not Urgent" area but I know how important it is for me to make sure that it doesn't slip into the "Not important" area again.

Whatever you discover or confirm, please don't use it as another reason to feel bad about your life. We can always take some baby steps towards a healthier and more balanced life. Finding out the negative consequences of keeping things as they are increases our motivation to take those baby steps to change. If you see the costs of what you are doing (to your health, happiness and wellbeing) and you also see what you could do instead, you can combine where you are moving FROM and where you are moving TO, which is powerful motivation not only for taking the first steps, but also to keep going!

BONUS CHALLENGE: why don't you create a relationship schedule with yourself? Add activities that are specifically aimed at strengthening your relationship with yourself to your day. Assign them a specific time slot and commit to having "minidates" with yourself. If you schedule "me-time" in your diary, you will be less likely to override it in favour of more "urgent" activities. It is also nice to plan in "spontaneous time", that is to say, to block out a segment of time in your week to do whatever your heart feels like at that time.

SELF-CARE TOOL #33: FRIENDS

What does friendship mean to you?

What role does friendship play in your life?

Do you consider yourself a good friend? Why? If not, what would you like to improve on?

Does friendship contribute to your wellbeing or does it seem like one more chore?

Do you have different friends for different activities?

Do you notice your friends have anything in common? For instance, do they all like to connect very frequently or only on special occasions? Do they all share an activity with you? Are they all old friends? Are they all fairly new friendships?

Would you like to make new friends? If so, where or how do you think you might meet some potential friends? Do you find it easy or difficult to let go of a friend, whether it is because they have died or because the relationship has gone cold?

In your current friendships, do you play an active role or do your friends tend to reach out to you and organise joint events?

Do you notice anything else with regards to your friendships?

Do you notice any similarities or striking differences between the way you show up in your friendships and the way you show up in your relationship with your spouse/partner? What does that mean to you?

SELF-CARE TOOL #34: WHEN YOU DON'T KNOW YOU CAN

Your prescription is to take care of yourself today

Today I gave myself permission to be myself and to do what I need to do to care for myself.

That act of giving permission seemed to go very deep. It seemed to go against things I had learned a long time ago. And there was a certain sense of expansion from knowing that I can give myself permission. I just didn't know I could.

Is there anything you want to give yourself permission to be, to feel, or to do? Taking full responsibility and checking that your actions won't cause any harm to yourself or others, can you give yourself permission?

Maybe you would like to give yourself permission to feel better right now, to feel more relaxed, to feel more vibrantly energised... Now you know you can.

SELF-CARE TOOL #35: DARING TO FEEL DEEPLY

I would save this one for a good day, a day when there is no turmoil around, when we are not rushed, unwell or particularly under pressure.

Sometimes somebody says something and our inner being gets shaken. We feel the "hit" really strongly. For me, it is as if I have a bruise in my knee and I keep banging that particular spot everywhere! There is a combination of the pain from the bruise and the pain from the new incident.

When it comes to emotions, if a word or action lands on an existing emotional wound, the pain gets magnified.

So my initial invitation, as a warm-up, is to be curious and observe what happens when we have a moment of emotional pain. Maybe we have received the arrow of a careless comment, so after doing what we need to do (maybe removing ourselves from that place until things calm down), let's try to shift our attention from the arrow to the place where it has landed. Is there an old wound there? Can we treat the arrow as a pointer to help us to find that old wound and tend to it?

That in itself is great work! Take your time over it.

And if you are brave enough to look into that wound, you will most probably end up in a more compassionate place within you.

There are all sorts of wounds, but there is one that is quite personal and tends to be overlooked. Here is a definition of how it feels:

> *"the intensely painful feeling or experience of believing that we are flawed and therefore unworthy of love, belonging, and connection"*

> (Brown, 2021, p. 137).

Have you ever felt that? In your relationship, perhaps? I have found it lurking under anger.

This is painful territory, so it is OK if you feel like closing the book right now. Just remember to come back when you are ready. We can go through this together.

I will share a very personal experience around this: one day I approached my husband to say good morning and get organised for the day (sometimes we do things together). He said good morning and gave me a meaningful kiss. I asked him whether we could organise our day. He asked me what I was going to do. I replied I had many things to do, and I was expecting work, probably in the afternoon... At this stage he was already walking to another room and doing something else. I said to him, "Hey, we were talking". He answered in what sounded like a very angry voice to me: "I have many things to do." Next, I saw him sucking one of his fingers. He had hurt himself. I checked and he told me he was not bleeding (it turned out to be a minor cut, with the sharp edge of a shelf). He told me he had no time for chatting. I left the room in silence. He had hurt his finger; I had a wound to tend to, too. (Mind you, it is not every time that I can keep calm and aware. Many times, the pain is so intense I feel I will explode if I don't let it out somehow, so I have to physically move, or I will get angry. Anger feels easier than this).

When I replayed the feelings in my mind as if they were in slow motion, I felt a hit in my chest. It felt as if I had received a blow with something large. It was not an intense pain. It was a heavy, dull pain. It felt dark, and it seemed to squeeze my chest. My eyes welled up.

I felt inferior, powerless, lonely, and humiliated, as if I had unknowingly done something wrong and the fact that I could not find what that wrongdoing was made me somehow flawed… I allowed myself to feel all of that.

I speak to other partners regularly, and I know I am not the only one who experiences this. Just knowing that other people go through this helps enormously when I feel alone and unworthy of connection like in this case.

I can also be with the feeling without getting stuck in it. The actual things that happened ("the story") tend to be gone from my mind at this stage. I feel more space. I can breathe freely, without the heavy feeling in my chest.

So I can reflect more. What is the feeling pointing to? Have I felt this before? It is a "knowing" that I am flawed and something is wrong in me and nobody should discover, a secret that cannot see the light and needs to be kept in silence. There is something I don't accept in myself and I know it feels like it is something very, very wrong. I am patiently getting closer.

If you recognise the experience, *it usually goes by the name of shame*. Shame thrives in the dark. When you bring it into the light, it tends to decrease rapidly. So if you can talk about it, you can really help yourself.

Even journaling about shame helps us bring it to the light, so if you feel something like this, next time do what you can to expose it in a safe environment.

Maybe you can write a letter to yourself about this feeling (not about what happened), or perhaps you can talk to a very trusted friend, your spiritual director, or a therapist.

SELF-CARE TOOL #36: TAKE THE LONG-TERM VIEW

If you feel overwhelmed by some current experience, can you pause and think about the journey that has brought you to the present, focussing in on your strength and resilience?

Can you think about previous "battles" you have fought, even those which involved unfortunate or unhealthy decisions or actions, and create space by thinking about how much you have progressed and what you have learned?

Can you feel some difference between the past you, who perhaps took a wrong turn then, and the present, wiser, you?

Can you focus more on who you are becoming rather than the lessons that your journey may be presenting right now?

Above all, try to avoid making choices based on the stress of immediacy and make a healthier, better choice for the long run.

SELF-CARE TOOL #37: AFFIRMATIONS

Sometimes, just repeating a phrase or affirmation is enough to top up our emotional or spiritual energy.

Here are some suggestions:

This is not personal. It is autism.

I am resilient and resourceful.

I can take a break when I need one.

Curious silence is the best solution right now.

I am my own cheerleader.

This storm will pass.

Love is always loving me.

When I know better, I do better.

In my world, everybody gets to make mistakes (including me).

Just remember that affirmations are not tools for denying what is happening and failing to take action. If a situation is not safe, I think that no amount of repetitions of "*I am safe and all is well in my world*" will work. Affirmations are not excuses. Affirmations are ways of acknowledging, reminding, and focussing on something that we may have overlooked or forgotten.

More at
The Companion You have a special page in The Companion for you to write down your own affirmations.

SELF-CARE TOOL #38: SAFE TIME-TRAVEL (TO THE PAST)

Revisiting the past may be helpful. It can allow us to review previous situations to get the learnings and understandings from those events that could help us in the now.

Many years ago, somebody told me that it is OK to time-travel in our heads. He said that the trick is in the contents of our backpack. I am very curious, so I asked him to tell me more. He then explained that when we decide to visit our "museum of memories", it is a good idea to pack some oil and some scissors. I was totally clueless as to what he meant.

He explained that it is a good idea to rub some oil onto ourselves before entering the museum because there are lots of memories stored there and we don't want anything we find in there to leave a "sticky" residue when we come out.

What about the scissors? Well, while we are in the museum, we may find some thick cobwebs we may want to cut through or we may develop some strong binding to our favourite stories, so we may decide to use the scissors to cut out ties with those moments in our lives. The scissors will remind us to acknowledge what happened, thank it for its contribution to our life (even if it was something awful that showed us how much we can go through), and cut the connection.

Museums have opening times, so we can't be there forever. We don't live at the museum. Before leaving the museum, just in case, it is a good idea to check our backpacks. We don't want to take anything that belongs in the museum with us!

On our way out, we can wipe any sticky memories off us easily with the help of the oil we applied before going in and check just in case the scissors come in handy to let go of something we feel particularly bound to. Then we are ready to come back to this very present moment and notice how we feel.

SELF-CARE TOOL #39: SAFE TIME-TRAVEL (TO THE FUTURE)

More at The Companion When I am time-travelling to the future, I like the setting to be as open and safe as possible.

I tend to choose one of my favourite places in nature, sometimes it is a beach I like, sometimes it is one of the waterfalls I have been to, sometimes it is a forest, sometimes it is a place I have only seen in my dreams at night.

You may want to leave the timeframe open, too, or you may want to set your intention to envision your future self in 5/10/20 years.

I like travelling light, so I don't prepare any backpacks for this trip.

I relax and when I feel I am in the future, I get curious about any changes I may notice in myself.

What does my future self look like?

What doubts, fears or worries have disappeared?

What new wisdom has arisen?

Is there any difference in the way I stand, behave, or sound?

Have my goals in life changed, or become clearer?

I may get a chance to ask my future self any questions. One I especially like is "which is the best way to prepare myself for a wiser version of myself in the future?"

Do I need to revise my values? Do I need to change or drop any behaviour? Do I need to take up new challenges? Do I need more rest?

When I am ready to go back to the present, I thank my future self. She doesn't like me to go empty-handed, so she will bless me with some parting message or give me a meaningful imaginary gift to remind me of this moment.

SELF-CARE TOOL #40: WHAT ARE YOUR VALUES?

Questions are such a powerful tool to reflect! Deep questions help us to examine ourselves, and they often challenge our beliefs about what we 'know' to be true.

More at The Companion In The Companion you will find a list of questions to help you explore your values, which are reproduced below, too.

Take time to work through the questions, which carefully put together many of the aspects already covered in previous tools, to gain further insight into who you are, what you believe and what you want in life.

There are a lot of questions so you could choose to do one or two a day.

To get started, why don't you pick a number between 1 and 50 and journal about the relate question that bears that number in The Companion today?

1) In what ways are you living outside of your integrity and compromising your personal values? In other words, do your actions and words support your personal values?

2) What have you left unfinished or unresolved that currently needs your attention?

3) What deep needs do you have that are not getting met?

4) What are you fighting against that you can choose to release?

5) What legacy are you leaving behind in the world after you've gone?

6) In what ways could you be more engaged in life?

7) In what ways are you behaving inauthentically?

8) Who (or what) are you tolerating that you do not want in your life?

9) How are you making choices based on 'I should' as opposed to 'I desire'?

10) In what ways are you reacting rather than initiating actions?

11) How are you failing to accept someone that you love for who they really are?

12) How do you diminish other people in order to make yourself feel better?

13) Are there any areas in which you are withholding forgiveness? Where?

14) In what ways are you manipulating someone to get your own needs met?

15) What consistent negative thought patterns do you have?

16) In what ways do you allow other people to cross your boundaries?

17) What weaknesses or vulnerabilities are you afraid to share with those you love?

18) How are you completely present with those that you love when you are with them?

19) In what areas do you have a 'lack' mentality?

20) In what areas are you making your own life more difficult or complicated than it needs to be?

21) Are your beliefs about life, religion, your partner, your family and your children the absolute truth?

22) In what ways are you using busyness, work, television, or the computer to avoid facing something?

23) How is your living space a reflection of your inner world?

24) In what ways are you compromising your health?

25) What are you passionate about? How can you spend more time pursuing the things you are passionate about?

26) In what areas of your life do you need to set flexible and realistic goals?

27) How have you miscommunicated or created a misunderstanding?

28) How much of your time do you spend focusing on things of the past or worrying about the future?

29) What events are you focusing on in the past that are hindering your ability to live fully in the present?

30) In what ways do you consider that you are not deserving or worthy?

31) What relationships need your time, care and attention?

32) In what areas are you waiting for someone else to take responsibility for you?

33) In what ways are you allowing fear of change to hold you back from moving forward in life?

34) In what areas are you spending too much time on things that are not your priorities?

35) In what areas do you need to learn or further develop skills in order to get ahead in life?

36) What would those close to you say your strengths are?

37) What would those close to you say your weaknesses are?

38) In what ways are you not taking responsibility for the part you are playing in a relationship problem?

39) How does your work reflect your interests, passions, skills?

40) Where are you prioritising money/material possessions over relationships and your values?

41) What are you allowing to distract you from living life to the fullest?

42) What is your vision for the next five years?

43) How are you helping other people to become better versions of them?

44) If you were to die tomorrow, what would you regret not having done?

45) In what ways are you living a life someone else has defined for you?

46) What is your intuition telling you that you might have been ignoring?

47) What really pushes your buttons that does not need to?

48) What drains your energy and in what ways can you change that?

49) In what ways are you being financially unwise or irresponsible?

50) In what areas are you so desperately longing for an outcome that it's preventing you from enjoying the journey?

SELF-CARE TOOL #41: WHAT DOES IT MEAN?

This self-care tool is, like the previous one, a complete workout in itself, so take your time…

…and use the space at The Companion if you find it helpful.

More at
The Companion

If we watch our mind carefully, we may find that it is like a meaning-making production unit. We see something or something happens and thoughts pop up to offer explanations as to the meaning behind that.

When we are little, it seems our minds are much more like a camera, taking everything in, but then we start asking "Why?" and the answers we get to those questions stay with us for a long time, somewhere in the basement room of our mind, out of our conscious awareness. Those are our beliefs.

If somebody says something meaningless about us (e.g. "You are a pink elephant"), we don't feel any powerful emotions.

EVENTS THAT HAVE NO MEANING CAN'T MAKE YOU FEEL ANYTHING

We create our beliefs to give meaning to things, to help us organise the learnings we store in our memory.

Some of those beliefs limit us and cause us pain (such as the common belief "I am not enough" or its opposite "I am too much", "I can't trust anybody", "Other people's criticisms are true" or "Other people are more important than me"), so it is beneficial to gradually become aware of them and question their validity in this stage of our lives.

Here are some questions to lead you gently through a discovery journey:

1) What is a problem or limitation that has held you back for a while?

2) What is it you would like to do/have, except something is stopping you getting it/doing it?

3) What is it that is REALLY stopping you from getting what you want?

4) This is a problem because...

5) And this means... (Repeat as many times as necessary)

6) What must you believe that makes this problem even exist?

7) What is it you believe about YOURSELF that has made this a problem?

8) What do you believe about the WORLD that has made this a problem?

8a) If there is another person involved, what do you believe about the OTHER PERSON that has made this a problem?

9) What is this problem an example of?

10) ...and what is THIS (*the answer to question 9*) an example of?

11) When did you decide that your problem was a problem (roughly)?

12) At what point in your life did you buy into this concept?

13) What decision did you make that caused this problem to be born?

14) What does this problem mean to you?

15) What will life be like when you don't have this problem? / What will that give you?

The good news is that...

WE CAN CHANGE THE MEANING EVENTS HAVE FOR US!

For instance, instead of believing that we are not good enough, we may decide to believe our primary caretakers may have had unrealistic expectations for us as a child.

Common self-limiting beliefs are:

- ❖ What makes me good enough and important is achieving things
- ❖ I'm not good enough
- ❖ I'm not important
- ❖ I'm not capable
- ❖ What makes me good enough is having other people think well of me
- ❖ Mistakes and failures are bad
- ❖ If I make a mistake or fail, I will be rejected/People won't like me if I make a mistake
- ❖ Other people's criticisms are true
- ❖ Love must be earned
- ❖ I don't deserve love and success
- ❖ My wants and needs should be sacrificed for others/Other people's wants and needs carry more weight than mine
- ❖ I must be loved and approved of to feel okay
- ❖ Other people's opinions carry more weight than mine
- ❖ Other people's opinions carry more weight than mine

❖ I'm only lovable if a partner loves me (or at least needs me)

Since we are the ones who give meaning to events and things, it is in fact us who create our beliefs, so now we can create better ones.

Revising and updating our beliefs helps us align our life more closely with the values we want to embody.

Our beliefs determine our habitual patterns. What we do, feel, or avoid depends on our habits.

Our beliefs affect all spheres of our lives.

When you are with your relatives, which beliefs seem to be underneath your behaviour? Are you the accommodating, self-sacrificing person in the family? Do you become silent and disappear from everybody's radar? Which beliefs would you think drive your behaviour when you are in family situations?

If you work or study, which role do you habitually take and which beliefs can you identify? Do you believe that everybody but you can be successful? (by the way, examining your own definition of success can point you to some interesting hidden beliefs). Do you believe you can't get anywhere unless you work hard/compete fiercely/know the right people on the business ladder?

When you are with your partner, what habits do you embody? Are you the devoted/emotionally-deprived/resentful husband/wife/boyfriend/girlfriend?

These are all habits. We reinforce them with repeated practice and they are probably based on a set of beliefs about ourselves, our family, the business world, the world at large, our partners, how relationships work, autism, etc.

As we have found, we are the ones who create meaning out of things. We create our beliefs, which later run our lives.

Therefore, we are the ones who can change our lives by changing our beliefs. Some people start by changing their habits, some others start by changing their beliefs. I particularly find that discovering core beliefs, finding where reality contradicts those beliefs and introducing baby steps in adopting new habits brings more consistent and long-lasting results.

This is so pivotal in our lives that I would like to invite you to **put things in writing, so that you can revisit them and amend as you go along**.

Here is an example of a simple table you may use:

Beliefs	Habits	New beliefs	New habits
e.g. My needs are not important.	I hyper-focus on what verybody else needs. I don't take enough rest.	I am willing to remember that my needs are as important as everybody else's.	I will trust other people have their own strength and skill to look after their needs. I will check my needs regularly during the day. I will take regular breaks and refrain from pushing on when I am too tired. I will ask for help when I need it.

So in the first column on the left, write down the hidden beliefs you have found with the help of this self-care tool (and any others you might have known already).

In the second column, write down the behaviours that come from each belief.

In the third column, rephrase the original belief so that it is healthier, but still achievable right now

In the far right column, write down what baby steps you can take towards new behaviours.

◆ ◆ ◆

DON'T FEEL GUILTY WHEN YOU DO SOMETHING FOR YOURSELF

◆ ◆ ◆

SELF-CARE TOOL #42: THE BIG WHY

I know that many times when things are not going so well in our relationship, we tend to wonder why we choose our partners. I would like to invite you to join me in exploring this because it is a key factor in helping you to know yourself more fully.

More at
The Companion There are many reasons (both conscious and unconscious) why we might choose a partner. Since this is an emotional subject for many of us, you will now see a list of options (also reproduced at The Companion). Mark all that apply, and feel free to add your own.

→ Were you going through an especially vulnerable time in your life when you met your partner? (I met my husband 4 years after my mother's death and about a month before my father's second marriage. I was in a relationship with a man who was still living with his ex-wife. I was an emotional wreck. Big tick for me! When I met the man who would become my husband two years later, he seemed so cool and calm. He spoke with such depth and conviction! And he was (still is) so handsome!!! I felt I could trust him. He was also into body-building, so he was physically strong and made me feel secure and protected in his presence.)

→ Did you see the potential in your partner when you met them? Deep inside, was it like a personal project in which you undertook to teach them something, make up for something in their lives, or fix something in them? (Hummm, yeah. I think I should tick this one, too.)

→ Did you see your partner as a good match for your values or for your vision of what a family should be like? (I think I did then, but then noticed he was not interested in having children, for instance. We had some important values in common, so I will give this a tick, too.)

→ In retrospect, do you think you might have experienced autistic-like traits within your family of origin? Maybe one of your parents displayed autistic-like behaviours? [This doesn't necessarily imply that there were autistic people in your family. Sometimes trauma causes similar behaviours.] (Tick for me.)

→ In retrospect, do you think you might have experienced high levels of anxiety within your family of origin? (Big tick for me.)

→ Was there something in your partner that seemed familiar to you apart from the autistic traits and anxiety? Did you perhaps get the feeling that you already knew this person? (I did!)

→ Did your partner have sweet little gestures during the dating period? (My husband used to read things to me. I loved that!!!)

→ Did you sense that being with your partner would help you grow as a person? (Another big tick for me. I thought he was much more evolved than me.)

→   Any other personal reasons?

When you have finished your honest exploration about what may have drawn you to this person, read what you have marked/ written and try to discover what unmet need or expectation you might have had. Put the focus back on you. Is that need in you still unmet? Are you still holding that expectation?

I think the summary of my findings here was that I saw him as a steady rock who would help me to carry the responsibilities of adult life and to process emotional wounds in me, as well as a person to whom I could teach new things.

Whatever your findings are... can you be or provide that for yourself instead of expecting your partner to be or provide that for you? Can you find a way to meet those needs or expectations (if they are still valid, and I suspect many will be) in a group or with friends? (We will revisit expectations in the next self-care tool. I know it is another biggie!)

SELF-CARE TOOL #43: EXPECTATIONS VERSUS CHOICE

Now we are ready to approach a topic that comes up very often in support groups for partners of people on the autism spectrum: expectations.

Expectations have been a challenge and source of pain for me. I battled for a long time against the expectations I (and my family) had of what a relationship should be versus the reality of what it is.

Even after my husband's diagnosis, I struggled to find out what expectations are realistic for us.

I have heard people say that if you are in a relationship with somebody on the spectrum you should drop all expectations. What do you think? Do you think your expectations sometimes lead to pain? Do you think you can have some expectations in your relationship or do you agree with those people who say we should apply a "zero expectations" rule?

More at
The Companion

Do you ever wish things were different? If your wishes mobilise and uplift you, it's OK. However, if your wishes lead you along a downward path that paralyses you and brings your mood down, this may be the time to stop and look for another way, especially if your wishes are in the area of your relationship with a person on the autism spectrum becoming more like what we see in traditional romantic films.

Oh, dear reader! I wish we could be sitting across a table with a cup of tea so that I could see your face when you read what I am going to type next.

I have compared my relationship to other relationships and more often than not, the result was not uplifting. Would you like me to share something that has helped me in this regard? Rather than trying to stop my mind engaging in comparative exercises –which, as I have said, hasn't worked for me– I would like you to consider the possibility of the wonderful opportunity our relationship brings as compared with those relationships where neurodiversity is not present (let's call them 'standard relationships' for short).

If you are in a standard relationship, you may compare what you have with your expectations, which are based on what you know from other couples, from other relationships, and from romantic movies and books, etc. If what you have matches your expectations to some degree, you feel satisfied. If it doesn't, you may feel there is something wrong in the relationship and try to shape what you have into that mould.

Is that really the way you want to live your life with your partner?

If your relationship is an important aspect of your life, do you really want it to follow a predefined template?

I hope you have answered these last two questions with a big 'NO!'

When there is neurodiversity in a relationship, we may still feel some pressure to fit into the conventional template, we may still have the same expectations…

Until we realise that the hidden blessing we get in our kind of relationships: there is no template!

We don't need to conform! We get to change our expectations and choose!

We get to decide what we are going to do in order to set up ourselves, our partners, and the relationship for success!

We even get to decide what success means for us. For some neurodiverse couples, success may mean doing some of the things people do in 'standard relationships' (such as going out on dates, having children, sleeping in the same bed or having a relatively active social life). For some of us, success may mean starting from scratch, getting to know what each of us brings to the table over time, and accepting that we may need to do many things without our partners or without our partners' support. It may also mean that our partners may need additional briefing, encouragement, time alone and reminding, or that we may need to attend family functions on our own, to mention a few.

I think it's a no-brainer really, but our emotions get in the way. At work, we may expect our partners' employers to make reasonable adjustments. Why not make reasonable adjustments in relationships, too?

How do you feel when you read this?

HOW LIBERATING!

WE ARE NOT MEANT TO FIT INTO THE STANDARD ROMANTIC MOULD!

WE ARE MEANT TO CREATE OUR OWN!

Stopping the pain that comes from unfulfilled expectations may be an important part of self-care for you. If so, you might want to sit with this new paradigm for a while.

Having said all this, I think there is a time to grieve for our unrealistic expectations, too. If you are in a situation where you are still struggling to let go of some expectations that you know cannot become a reality in your relationship, it may be that the path is through feeling the pain not running away from it (perhaps you already secretly suspect that deep down). To do this, we need to create a little space around the pain by reminding ourselves that there are also positives in our relationship and in our life outside the relationship.

Try this exercise (which you will find in The Companion with plenty of space for you to reflect on). Write down all the expectations you have of your relationship. Sort them into ones that cause suffering and ones that don't.

Next, write down all the reasons for letting go of your romantic expectations and creating your relationship as if it were a painting on a white canvas, having freedom of choice in order to make it specifically tailored for the two of you.

I find this exciting. Do you?

If you struggle to envisage how to create a fulfilling relationship between you two, you may consider revisiting your needs as an individual and also getting to know what you need in the relationship that you can realistically get. Alternatively, you may continue to Part 2 and come back here after you have found out more about your partner and how to create an environment where meaningful communication can happen.

PART 2:
COMMUNICATION

Your pillars for communication

The first part of your journey with the help of this book was focussed on you. Now we are ready to look at the part of our relationships where we tend to find most deficits: communication.

This chapter will take you into a process of gradual discovery around your personal styles of communication in the relationship and the main challenges you may be experiencing. It may help you stay curious and discover more things about your partner/spouse.

I would like to share something that happens in my relationship: if I share from a vulnerable place, my husband listens to me and responds accordingly. Now, my problem with regards to this is that for many years I thought that being vulnerable was venting my feelings freely on my husband. Later on I realised that being vulnerable requires being in touch with my deeper emotions and communicating those in a safe manner. You may want to pause here and reflect about how vulnerable you allow yourself to be with your husband these days. Misunderstandings and resentments may, over time, disconnect us from our vulnerable side.

I must admit that my dream communication with my husband would look like the following photo...

I am highly emotional and I find many things to be interested in. I have a BA in teaching and I am very enthusiastic about sharing what I learn and discover, as well as what matters to me. It is logical for me to want to share that with my husband.

However, over the years we have been together, I have seen that many times, my husband doesn't share my level of enthusiasm about most things. In fact, he rarely does.

I have realised that when I approach my husband with a view to sharing, what he experiences is more like the following ominous scene:

So, logically, my approach is not that welcome and he does this:

Does this sound familiar, dear reader?

First things first. If you struggle with communication in general and tend to either become overly passive or aggressive rather than assertive, you may benefit from improving your overall communication style. There are many valuable online resources on assertiveness, non-violent communication, and useful communication tools.

In this part of our journey together we will explore communication and different specific aspects of communication that may be present in our relationships. This will help you to take an honest look at your communication style (and the one best suited to your partner), their strengths, their weaknesses, and any blindspots in order to understand why many times communication might feel like walking through a minefield which doesn't achieve anything positive for anybody. It will also help you to find a new level of connection through adapting the ways in which you communicate.

We will start by looking at some generic situations we may face:

DIFFERENT OVERALL STYLES WHEN WE ARE NOT TRIGGERED

In your communications with your partner, do you tend to communicate in a logical way, giving objective information and exact data, which reflects "the truth"? Or do you tend to communicate in an emotional way, seeking connection, looking to be happy rather than being right? Does your partner tend to communicate in the same way?

Can you find a common ground between the styles that come more naturally to you? (In my case, the common ground is usually related to my husband's special interests).

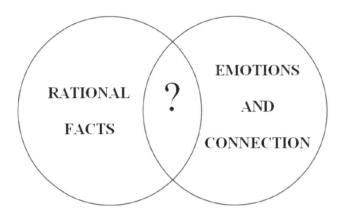

Do you tend to use concrete facts or do you like painting pictures with your words, using more abstract language, such as metaphors? Does your partner tend to communicate in the same way?

Do you use absolutisms (that is to say, expressions such as always or never)? Is it one or both of you? Does one have the tendency to use absolute language and then the other starts using the same style, too? Be curious and try to notice that when/if it happens.

When there is something to be resolved, do you tend to insist that you need to discuss it/find closure? Or do you try to shove it under the rug and avoid difficult conversations? Is your partner avoidant or insistent?

Do you think you can understand your partner's point of view most of the time? Do you think your partner can understand yours? Some people refer to the double empathy problem, which I understand as a situation in which person A can't empathise with person B and person B, in turn, struggles to empathise with person A. In other words, it is not just that the autistic person struggles to empathise with the neurotypical person. The opposite is also true, the neurotypical person has such a different perception, understanding, lived experience and way of dealing with things, that they would also need to make an effort to empathise with the autistic person. I imagine this is similar to two people who are enveloped by thick fog, in which both struggle to see the full picture and will fill in the blanks with what they know.

Just because some styles may come naturally to you, it doesn't necessarily follow that they are the best for your particular relationship either. Is there anything you have noticed already that you would like to change or improve on your side of the communication?

More at
The Companion

ADDITIONAL CHALLENGES TO COMMUNICATION

Importance: before embarking into a passionate conversation about something with our autistic partner/spouse, it is very useful to pause and check how important that topic (really) is for us or for the relationship.

Is it really worth raising at all with our partner, or is it something we can let go of or talk to somebody else about? If we are not sure about the degree of importance, we can ask ourselves whether it affects our lives to a significant degree.

We may even imagine traffic lights to convey what action we want to take according to how important the topic is:

Not important at all.
Stop!

Not so important. Wait or proceed with caution.

Important enough for me or the relationship. We might need to schedule a good time for both.

Timing: you have probably worked out already that it is not a good idea to start a conversation that is important for you when your partner is engaging in their special interest or thinking about something else.

Processing: Does your partner need extra processing time? Unless it is a vital emergency, consider adjourning the conversation before reaching a final outcome. A few minutes may be enough. Sometimes you need to agree on a later date to carry on. I tend to say I need a tea or loo break when I notice he is thinking hard.

Interruptions: Does one of you interrupt the stream of words and thoughts from the other and takes it in a different direction? How does it feel to be on the receiving end of such an abrupt episode of abandonment? What meaning do we attach to that?

More often than not, it is simply a sign of misunderstanding or incomplete information. The listener interrupts in order to clarify meaning and if they are not sure about what the topic or main point of the message was, they may try one or several possible topics. It is painful and frustrating. If the speaker wants to continue the conversation in a civilised manner, the best way forward is to rephrase the previous message and check that it is understood.

Mind-reading: Do you ever feel you know your partner's intentions? Does your partner ever tell you they know your intentions? When we make assumptions, we may end up assigning a deliberate intention where none was present. If you are going to assume an intention, then it is healthier to assume a positive one. It is better still to check instead of assuming.

Blaming or criticism: It is much easier to hear "constructive" criticism or blame from anybody than from the people who are closest to us. It sometimes feels as if they are rejecting who we are and we may go into shame as a result. Do you tend to criticise your partner's actions? If they sense criticism, they may stop doing things for you.

Do you get criticised by your partner? Listen carefully to them. I have noticed that many times, what comes out as criticism against me is just a reflection of what my husband is telling HIMSELF at that moment. In other words, he may be criticising himself, but it comes out as being aimed at me. Sometimes he puts his hands in mine and says "cold hands" as if he were referring to mine, but my hands are warm and his are cold. Unfortunately, his tone of voice and inflection may be very misleading!

It may be that he is replaying what somebody told him when he was little. Check. Is your partner blaming you for things that he/she has done or for the consequences of his/her actions, perhaps? Is your partner blaming you for anything and everything? I know it is difficult not to get reactive in the moment, we are all humans and hurtful words hurt. However, could you perhaps entertain the possibility that instead of reacting you could focus on your partner's state when he/she says those hurtful things? What can you see? Does your partner look anxious, angry, tired, sad, or hungry? It is normally not about us, it may just be their way of expressing (that is to say, showing outwardly) that they are feeling a strong emotion inside and they don't even know what it is.

Of course, if there is some truth in what your partner is saying, it may be a helpful pointer towards change in you, but the main strategy is to find ways to become interested in his inner world. This in turn will help us prevent reactive behaviours we may regret later. Just be curious. I sometimes imagine myself picking up a magnifying glass and looking for clues, as if I were a detective. Please note that this doesn't mean interrogating your partner in any way; it means being open, curious, and as objective as possible so that you can find a plausible answer to the question 'What is really going on here?'.

Whether it seems truthful or totally unrelated to you, aim at getting to a stage where you don't react. Your partner may be processing something. No matter what they have said, focus on the <u>EMOTION</u> that may be driving such an attitude, not on the message or behaviour. It is much more helpful to think "Oh, my partner is anxious, frightened, tired, hot, hungry, or distressed because of the noise, environment, workload, etc." than to keep ruminating on "I am not xyz. He is so..." If this sounds unthinkable right now, don't worry. We still have many steps to take on this journey together!

Perceived blame or criticism causes so much heartache in relationships that I would like to invite you to reflect a bit more about this. Either or both of you can feel blamed or criticised at any given moment.

There are two important concepts in the previous statements: 'perceptions' and 'feel'. The word 'perception' can be used to express a way of regarding, understanding or interpreting something, in other words, a mental impression of external stimuli. It can also mean the process of becoming aware of something through the senses. In both cases, this word describes a process that involves an experiencer, not a fact that is known to be true.

So, criticism and blame can be a perception. Somebody may be interpreting something the other party says as criticism, but their intention may be just to help us improve (spoiler alert: our partners may have a tendency towards perfectionism). Being compassionate and extending grace goes a long way, so if at all possible, try to open to the possibility that your partner's intention may not be to criticise or blame.

What I find helpful (when I remember), is to imagine that the person who is seemingly blaming or criticising is like a pressure cooker, that has reached boiling point and has to let the steam out or else it will explode.

I don't know anybody yet that would feel blamed or criticised by the steam that is coming out of the pressure cooker. It is a good thing that the valve is working properly and letting the steam out. If it wasn't working properly, the results would be messy and dangerous. The steam is alerting us of the heat and pressure inside the cooker. It is an innocent messenger. In a similar manner, if we feel like saying (or if we blurt out) words that amount to blame or criticism, those words are letting us and others know that there is an unmet need or that we have betrayed ourselves and gone beyond our values or boundaries or simply that we have reached boiling point emotionally! If we are at the receiving end, our partners may be unable to identify 'what is cooking' inside them, but they have reached a point when they can't hold it in any more. They are sending an SOS message. They are not blaming or criticising us. They need time alone. Even though it is never helpful to interrogate them, sometimes it helps if we give them options about what to do next. For instance, yesterday I noticed that my husband was showing signs of overwhelm while we were designing something together that he wanted. I stopped and asked him whether we were looking at too many options and he was feeling lost. I suggested moving on and coming back to it later. That seemed to be the cue he needed to check with himself, so he paused and then he said 'No. I want to carry on.' He was calmer. I don't know exactly why. My guess is that he was feeling it was all getting out of control and my question made him realise he still had control over what to do next.

Defensiveness: When my husband starts asking me for a detailed report of the facts around a casual comment I have made, I get very defensive and I disconnect. I am trying to make a point and he is interrupting the flow!!!

When he gives me unsolicited advice, I get very defensive. Do you get defensive, too? Does your husband get defensive? In my opinion, the important thing is not whether we get defensive or not. What matters most is what we do or say when we get defensive. Often things can turn nasty, either blocking the communication or going in the direction of an argument. What

works for me is to notice when somebody is getting defensive and flag it in my mind. Then I just stop talking, feel the tension in my body and breathe deeply. It tends to work. If I am pressing my husband for action/an answer while he is not budging and getting defensive, stopping like this calms me down, enough to understand that it is not the right time for us to continue. It also gives my husband time to calm down and respond better.

Hidden agendas: Do you start your conversations with a very specific outcome in mind? This may narrow down your possibilities of finding out your partner's point of view on this, as well as the chances of getting an even better outcome you had not thought about. On the other hand, you may start a conversation about topic A when in fact, what you really want is to feel protected or seen by your partner. If that is the case, you increase the chances of getting what you want if you ask for it.

Do you tend to adopt a **specific role** in conversations with your partner? There are many ways to look into this. One is to check whether you are seeing yourself and your partner as adults or whether one is adopting a parental role and the other is adopting the role of a psychological child. By this I mean that once I adopt a parental role, my partner will tend to become either a rebellious or compliant child. This takes me into parental feelings such as over-responsibility, care-taking, or criticism. We stop relating to each other as fully functioning adults and start playing psychological games. Ideally, we should approach each other as soul-mates not as parent/child. If you are interested in this topic, you can research Eric Berne's ego states in Transactional Analysis.

You can also check whether you tend to adopt a specific role when you face conflict. Stephen B. Karpman was the first one to describe "the Drama Triangle". In his model, when we are under pressure in any way we may take up one of three complementary psychological roles: victim, rescuer, or perpetrator. Briefly, the victim is in a position of helplessness, so, for instance, the victim will complain or pretend incompetence so that they don't have to deal with things that seem too difficult. That's where the rescuer comes into play. The rescuer tends to fix, give solutions, and basically do things to take over responsibility from others. The rescuer wants to feel needed, wanted, or liked. Lastly, the perpetrator (or persecutor) is the one who blames, puts down, or criticises others to get what they want. Do you recognise any of these in yourself?

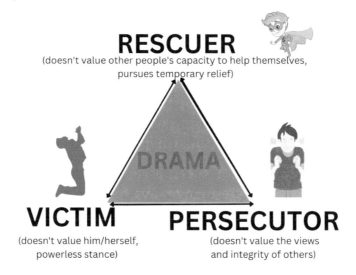

RESCUER
(doesn't value other people's capacity to help themselves, pursues temporary relief)

DRAMA

VICTIM
(doesn't value him/herself, powerless stance)

PERSECUTOR
(doesn't value the views and integrity of others)

Can you identify any dominant role in your partner? If you believe they are adopting an unhealthy role, rather than telling them, try not to adopt the opposite role while working to shift from your dominant role. For instance, if you tend to veer towards victimhood, it would be helpful for you to shift towards vulnerability by becoming more self-aware and learning problem-solving skills. If you tend to adopt the rescuer role, it would be helpful to shift towards a caring attitude by listening more and also being more self-aware. If you tend to adopt the perpetrator role, it is better to shift towards assertiveness. At the very least, try to stay in your adult state and to avoid the three roles of victim, rescuer and perpetrator. I have observed that my husband seems to pick up the hidden agenda in me very easily, even though I may not be aware of it. It is only when I see his reaction that I realise "Oh, he must have sensed I was trying to get him to do such and such. I had not realised I was trying to manipulate him! I didn't know it, but he did."

We all have some blind spots, and it is OK if we start recognising some things we do that may hinder our communication, the important thing is not to be too hard on ourselves.

We just don't know our blind spots are there, but when we explore the factors that may be affecting our communication, it is as if we are shining a bright torch and we may dispel a few of them. We can see more clearly, and we can make new choices.

Apart from differences in style and other overall challenges we may face, autistic traits may create specific situations with regards to communication.

We are now going to embark on a more specific, step by step, exploration of autism and communication.

The first step will be a reflection that can be very powerful, so allow enough time to let it sink in.

EXPLORATION #1: EMPATHIC REFLECTION

Let's put our empathy to work for a moment. Try to imagine you are your partner and reflect about the following questions **AS IF YOU WERE YOUR PARTNER/SPOUSE (NOT YOURSELF)** right now…

There are no right or wrong answers.

Just take your time until you find your honest answer to each of the questions.

More at
The Companion   What do I like about being on the autistic spectrum?

What do I dislike about being on the autistic spectrum?

As a person on the autistic spectrum, what do I believe is true about neurotypical people?

After answering those questions, you can continue reflecting from your own perspective.

How do you feel right now?

Do you think this reflection can help you in your communication to your partner? Why? / Why not?

EXPLORATION #2: THE SECRET GIFT OF STAYING CALM

Many people on the autism spectrum experience incredible amounts of stress. They are using a lot of "brain-power" to process everything that is going on. Imagine trying to compute lots of different bits of information in great detail at the same time! They are trying to come up with the right response to the situation knowing that in the past things turned nasty for them when they didn't (they got ridiculed, excluded, bullied, etc.)

If we stay calm, firstly we can remember all the things we know about autism.

We can remember that we are trying to stay connected with our partners, not to antagonise them.

We can even envisage the possibility of giving up the need to be right in order to be harmonious.

The great pay-off is that staying calm will eventually help our partners to calm down, too. If we are tense, they feel there may be some danger around and they feel unsafe. If we keep our cool, at least we won't be adding fuel to the fire.

EXPLORATION #3: MANY PEOPLE ON THE AUTISM SPECTRUM STRUGGLE TO GENERALISE THEIR LEARNING

This has been a tough one for me to get. My husband can do something in one context (say, at work) but it is painfully impossible for him to even imagine how to do it in another context (say, at home). So I remind myself that his brain is a bit like a fragmented hard disk. He does have the information somewhere, but it takes him a long time to put all the bits of information together… or he may fail to do so because he may be too stressed and it is as if the information is locked away and temporarily inaccessible.

What he learns in one context remains in his mental file for that context unless he makes the conscious effort to try to connect the different contexts. As I have heard somebody say "My partner can beat eggs for a cake, but if I ask him to beat eggs for an omelette, he asks me for instructions as if he had never done it before."

For those people who struggle to generalise what they have learned, their skills are not transferable from one context to the other until they make a conscious connection or a new rule. It is as if every new learning requires an overall reconfiguration of their knowledge. We will explore this further later.

EXPLORATION #4: NON-VERBAL WAYS TO COMMUNICATE

Even though our partners may speak fluently, there may be things that are difficult or quite painful for them to express. Sometimes we can help them by asking them to express how they are feeling by picking a song that reflects the mood, or to select a painting. The most artistic people might even perform their own songs or produce their own drawings or paintings.

There are different tools, such as cards, available on the market to help people express their emotions. I have bought Margot Sunderland's The Emotion Cards (Sunderland and Armstrong, 2018) and I have a story to tell around this.

On a Sunday afternoon a few years ago, my husband was obviously upset but I couldn't tell what was going on. I gave him the cards and asked him to pick one that expressed how he felt. He was going through the cards, putting one or two aside until he picked one and announced "This one!"

I was surprised to see he had handed me the following one.

Knowing, tender and kind

I was still puzzled. I asked whether he meant the words or the drawing. He acknowledged he had not seen the words... and added "That's us!"

I cherish moments like that one!

EXPLORATION #5: PLANNING YOUR CONVERSATIONS GOES A LONG WAY

As you may already know, it is not a good idea to start a conversation when our partners are transitioning from one activity to another one, such as when they have just arrived home from work or got up.

If we notice they are already focussing on something else, it is not the best time to speak to them either. Some people on the spectrum struggle to get back to what they were doing after an interruption. It is better to let them finish.

It is very helpful for me to imagine that my husband is diving and he is at great depth. It would be a shock for him to resurface quickly because he will be going through many different degrees of pressure. He needs to come up gradually, at a pace that feels safe for him.

The same happens when our partners are focussing one-pointedly on an activity and they need to shift focus to us. They need to take their time.

In my personal experience, the best time to speak to my husband is when he opens the conversation himself. I may say to him that I would like to speak to him about something that is important for us both or that I would like to hear his opinion about something. I may say that it would be nice to speak about it calmly. I may even give him a preview of the subject matter in one or two words. I may indicate whether it can or can't wait until the weekend/the next bank holiday, etc. And then I drop the subject. Any "nagging" will bring up his defences and escalate into a non-productive argument.

Using short sentences and pausing a lot whilst expressing what I want to say goes a long way. It helps me keep calm and assertive. It helps the message come out as a request, not a demand. I would like to think it also helps him see that it is really important for me. He knows that a happy wife makes his life much more comfortable. There is a gain for him in agreeing to have the conversation. He may suggest a suitable time himself. I put it down in writing so that he doesn't forget.

Of course, the best time to take swimming lessons/teach somebody to swim is not when we/they are drowning (this phrase is based on a quote by David Pitonyak. More on this on EXPLORATION #15).

Up until we scheduled a fixed weekly time for us to be together and catch up, things would build up and conversations would not go anywhere. Sunday afternoons are now "our time" and he has learned to ask me whether there is something specific I want to chat about. Sometimes we just watch a video (he gets points much better if they are not personal), sometimes we sit and plan. Many times the conversation turns towards something he is really interested in.

One thing I would like to share is that in our case, chats can't take up a whole afternoon. One of us will end up exhausted. If he is laser-focussed on something, at some stage I will say I need a cup of tea and head to the kitchen. If I see he is showing signs of irritability, loss of focus, anxiety, I say it may be better to park the subject for a while and I go somewhere else for a few minutes. This gives him a break to recover. Interestingly, many times when the focus on the conversation disappears, he realises that he is cold, or he needs a wee, and once he has seen to that need, he may be ready to continue the chat.

It is worth observing how your partner deals with internal signals of bodily needs. Some autistic people have difficulty recognising such signals and I imagine that for them it must be like they have a loud alarm going and they can't identify where it is from, let alone turn it off! No wonder they may get distracted and upset in some way. It is not personal.

EXPLORATION #6:
THE 8 SECOND PAUSE

KEEP 8 SECOND GAPS

My husband says he feels he has a slower mental processor than mine. He sometimes tells me he has heard the beginning of messages and he is still processing the rest. The way he describes it makes me think of the way some subtitles are scrolled at the bottom of a screen: subtitles go slower than speech; some parts may be either distorted (if the captions are auto-generated) or summarised (subtitlers need to shorten or simplify the message to allow for reading time); and it is difficult to remember the beginning of a sentence that you read on a previous screen.

Of course, when you are reading the subtitles, you also tend to miss all the action, all the cues from movement, body language, how things are said, etc., which tends to be an issue for our partners as well.

I have heard Dr Temple Grandin say that it would help us understand what it is like for autistic people if we imagined we are talking over a very poor phone line or internet connection and we have to wait for the message to reach the other end.

So if you want to give your partner a chance to get your whole message properly, pause for at least 8 seconds after each meaningful unit of information. I will be good for you, too. It will give you a chance to see the impact of your message and it will also give you a breather if you are getting carried away and need to calm down.

EXPLORATION #7:
ONE-WORD OR
VISUAL CUES

We all have our dominant way of experiencing life. When it comes to thinking, there seem to be two main trends: some of us think in words, some think in images (there is a third possibility, which sometimes co-occurs with autism, called synaesthesia, in which, for instance, words or thoughts are experienced as colours, sounds, smells, or tastes). It is worth becoming aware of our own prevalent way of thinking... and that of our partners'. Once we know their main cognitive route, we can use it when we need to use cues to remind them of things.

If our partners have to go through some written information, how do they go about it? Do they look at the illustrations first? This may be an indication that they tend to use images in their thinking process, however, it may also be related to reading difficulties, such as in the case of people with dyslexia. In order to check, look at how they are with charts and diagrams. Do they understand them at a glance? Do they need to read the key or text to get their meaning? In the latter case, they may still be relying more on words than images for their thinking.

I definitely think in images and I know that given a chance, I will go for the charts and graphics first. They show me how things fit into place. They give me the gist. My husband is very visual and goes for the images because he finds them attractive and cognitively knows they are helpful, but many times he struggles to make sense of charts and tables. So there is no point in me going all artistic and drawing cues to remind him of something. He might not be able to decode them.

A one-word cue may work for some people, not for him. He needs a phrase, such as "dentist today at 10.30", "I am doing such and such this afternoon", etc.

THERE IS
NO POINT
IN LEAVING MESSAGES
FOR OUR PARTNERS
IF THEY CAN'T
UNDERSTAND THEM!

A couple of very useful code words I have heard specialists recommend in neurodivergent couples' therapy are "Support" and "Strategy". Alternatively, we can use words such as "Comfort" and "Solution", respectively. If we want to tell our partners about something and we want to be listened to without them having to fix anything, we can use the word Support. When instead we are asking them for help or their opinion, we can ask them for a Strategy. Of course, as in the case of other kinds of messages, we need to make sure our partners understand the two terms before using them. I am not at this stage of sophistication yet. Right now, we are at the stage when I sometimes ask my husband just to listen to me, without helping or I ask him for his opinion or suggestion/help.

◆ ◆ ◆

EXPLORATION #8: JUST BECAUSE SOMEBODY IS GOOD AT TALKING IT DOESN'T NECESSARILY MEAN THEY ARE EQUALLY GOOD AT LISTENING

This has been a big realisation for me. My husband engages in conversation and he is knowledgeable and convincing, yet, if I listen closely, what he says may not be related at all to what he has been asked. He may be resuming a topic in the conversation that was dropped quite a while ago, or may even be recycling the points that somebody else made earlier. He says things in such a way that you would believe they are fresh and totally related to the topic in hand, though.

I think recycling points that somebody else has said before like this and presenting them as his own happens because of something called *echolalia* (even though it has not been diagnosed in my husband's case). Sometimes he will repeat a phrase over and over, but most often than not, he displays this kind of "delayed playback" of something he has heard.

As you can imagine, this causes problems. Before I spotted this, I thought he was gas-lighting me, because he would repeat something I had proposed and I took that as a sign of agreement. I then found out I had got the wrong end of the stick. I think it is more like a trance-like playback, not necessarily something he has processed or is aware of. If this sounds familiar, it is better to check that your partner really means what is coming out of their mouths.

See if they have a tendency to try to appease by claiming to understand even when that is not the case.

If they don't mean what they say, it doesn't necessarily follow that they are winding you up or gas-lighting you. It may be an instance of echolalia and it won't happen only with you; it may also be evident and create a problem at their workplace or in a social setting.

You may also notice that sometimes your partner struggles to give a coherent, logical and sequential description when they speak. It is not on purpose. I find that if I manage to calm and ask my husband short sequential questions, I can get what he means. Sometimes I need to say something like "I am getting confused about who did what. Let's slow down. I understand this far (and I summarise). Is this what happened?"

EXPLORATION #9:
HELPING THEM
FEEL SAFE

As you can imagine from everything we've discussed so far, your partner/spouse may have many reasons to feel unsafe.

I would like to add another layer of this never-ending onion: he/she may have been shamed or have felt inferior at school or at home and may have internalised this feeling of being less than other people.

Being different doesn't just lead to misunderstandings. In many cases, it has also led to being bullied, rejected, and/or taken advantage of.

Please don't take me wrong. I don't mean they are victims because from my perspective that is not a very empowering way to see things. I mean they have gone through a lot.

Most of them are real heroes who are unable to put their sagas into words.

That is why I propose helping them feel safe in as many ways we can, depending on their unique personal profile. It goes a long way.

For some people, safety may take the form of lower sensory triggers, prevention of last minute changes, simplified communication, written agreed schedules, and reminders before the time to switch to another activity, etc. Stay curious and find out the specific form safety may need to take in your home.

EXPLORATION #10: UNDERSTANDING WHY THEY DO WHAT THEY DO

As part of our "detective work", it may help to write down our findings as well as those things that puzzle us and we can't understand. If something has prevented communication, such as when there has been an episode of shutdown or meltdown, write as much as you can about the circumstances around it. It may take you a while, but once you have gathered enough data like this, you will most likely start discovering patterns, like "Oh, he always shuts down when he needs to go to the loo and he is confused about what his body signals mean."

EXPLORATION #11: ANY CHANGE DESTROYS THE WHOLE

Have you ever played Jenga, the game with the pile of blocks? I think my husband's brain is a bit like that. If you introduce one little change, it is like removing the block that brings the whole pile down.

Changes are very disruptive for most people on the autism spectrum. I used to be able to see that that was the case but I couldn't understand why changes (even those that were expected and scheduled beforehand) were so disruptive until I learned that people on the spectrum tend to see things as a whole (as Gestalts). When a minor detail changes, the resulting whole also changes in its entirety for them and they need time to "rebuild" that new reality.

For them it is not a little change, it is the collapse of a reality that had taken them a long time and endless patience to put together. So please use all your empathy to understand your partner's upset if this affects your communication. It is very logical from their point of view. Give them safe space to process their loss.

EXPLORATION #12:
BLUEPRINTS

We all have an internal blueprint, a kind of lens through which we view our experiences, which is based on the solid foundations of what we learned during our early years.

Research on the brain suggests that the brain can change, adapt, and learn new things constantly - that is called neuroplasticity. We know, therefore, that we can change if we are willing and able to undertake some conscious work on that blueprint, but we can only do that for ourselves. We can't expect our partners to want to become aware of their blueprints and work on them.

How do our blueprints affect our relationships?

Well, if for instance our husbands come from a family in which the male is the head of the family, who should not be disturbed or distressed at any time, and who gets to set all the rules in his "kingdom" but at the same time is not bound by those rules himself, they will have either adopted the same model as children or rebelled against it. They may have internalised that model and made it part of their blueprint.

During the initial phases of our relationship that blueprint may not be too evident for us, but sooner or later it will be a clear factor in our relationship.

It is worth looking at our own blueprint and trying to work out our partner's. Are they the same? Are they exact opposites?

162

Our partner's blueprint may manifest, for instance, in the way they express love to us.

Your partner probably didn't get unconditional love because his parents didn't know that he was on the spectrum and that he needed some adaptations for that. The first experiences of love in our partner's life (usually from parents or primary caregivers) may have included criticism, shaming, anxiously watching over the child's every move... so that is what we get in our relationship, too.

They don't mean to undermine our self-esteem, drive us crazy, dissect our experiences or make us uncomfortable by trying to notice our "imperfections" (in comparison to their blueprint) and exposing them in painful detail so that we can improve. They are serving us the dishes that are on their menu.

This is one of the discoveries which has spared me lots of unnecessary suffering. When I started noticing this, I would think "Who is he talking to? He is not talking to me." It was as if he had left me (and I don't like being abandoned!!!) and was replaying an old film in which he was talking to his mother.

I don't think I was born to fit into my husband's mental mould, but I can accept that he has one, that he is free to look into it and do things to update it with new values and rules or not. I can also accept that when my husband expresses something (maybe even his love) from his blueprint, I don't need to do anything about it. He is whistling his tune, I don't need to shut him off. I don't need to defend myself. In a way, it is like computer programming. There may be some features in a programme which help us do what we want to do, and there may be others that insist on doing things in a way that is not intended. We may get frustrated, but we don't feel offended/shamed/victimised, etc. etc. by the computer.

We can take our partners' "blueprint moments" as expressions of high anxiety. Communication cannot happen when either of us has been taken over by our blueprints. We need to pause the conversation, take time out and agree to continue when we are free from the automatic programming which our blueprints run in our heads.

EXPLORATION #13: WE ALL NEED TIME TO SELF-REGULATE

As we have already seen from different angles, we not only need to self-care for our own sakes, we also need to manage our emotions and keep calm for our partners' sake and for the sake of our relationship.

If we are triggered, it is better to take time out, chill out, and face whatever it is we need to face again.

The same holds true for our partners. If they are triggered, we can't expect them to even hear what we are saying or to give us a logical or meaningful answer.

EXPLORATION #14: MELTDOWNS AND SHUTDOWNS

When we are overwhelmed, it is as if we experience a build-up of energy inside us. The problem for some autistic people is that they may not be aware of the build-up as it is happening and end up with a fully blown explosion (meltdown) or implosion (shutdown). In general, children tend to have more meltdowns and adults tend to have more shutdowns.

So congratulations! If you have been noticing less meltdowns and more shutdowns in your partner, it means they are maturing. It doesn't mean they love you any less.

In either case, we can help by making sure our partners are safe, giving them plenty of space so that they can't get hurt and they can't hurt anybody, keeping as silent and calm as possible and trying not to move much. We know this will pass and they will be OK. They probably don't remember that at that stage, so try not to join them in their emotional turmoil.

Sometimes even walking towards them may make them feel more threatened. So stay where you are, relax your muscles, and soften your facial expression (especially, soften the area around your eyes if you can). If you need to speak, consciously lower your tone and volume. No brisk movements. If you must, imagine you have a huge wounded and starving grizzly bear in front of you!

EXPLORATION #15: "WHEN A PERSON IS DROWNING, THAT IS NOT THE BEST TIME TO TEACH THEM TO SWIM" (DAVID PITONYAK)

When I heard that quote for the first time, something inside me went "Ouch!" For some reason I cannot understand, when my husband is getting upset, I seem to become a fitness instructor and shout instructions at him. Of course, I am trying to be helpful, but the effect is the opposite. He shuts down.

The quote from David Pitonyak stops me in my tracks... if I remember it in time.

It works as a reminder that when my husband is getting upset, he needs his companion and not a dictator.

He needs a calm tone of voice, not shouting. He needs to see me smile, not scowl. He needs to see open body language, not a threatening finger in his face.

I know it is not easy for many reasons. For instance, we may have grown up in a family where raging was common. Or we may feel our partner's emotions in our body and get affected by them. Or perhaps we may need time out to self-regulate and our partner will follow us everywhere.

However difficult it may be, the sea can get too choppy for your partner. You may have to throw them a lifebuoy.

◆ ◆ ◆

EXPLORATION #16: MANAGING EXPECTATIONS AND SUSPENDING JUDGEMENT

In case you haven't read about expectations in Part 1, or as a reminder, as well as our blueprints, we all seem to come to relationships with expectations. These may be from previous romantic relationships, from other interpersonal relationships, from Hollywood films or Disney stories, for instance. Such expectations may be about something positive or negative.

It would be useful to stop and explore the ones you know you are holding. For instance, do you expect to be abandoned, cherished, betrayed, disappointed, ridiculed, told what to do, served like a princess, or treated like the housekeeper?

Do you expect your partner to be the home provider and to be able to fix a dripping tap?

Do you expect all the chores to be carried out by yourself/your partner?

Do you expect co-parenting?

Do you expect a good partner to be able to listen empathically to you and support you when you are not well?

For a long time, I believed that managing expectations was fighting against what I wanted/needed in order to avoid possible disappointment. We have explored this in ourselves in Part 1. Spoiler alert: It didn't work.

What works for me is to take an honest look at what is going on, not in the heat of the moment, but when I have some quiet time (alone or with a really good friend). What do I really want or need? Now you could also use the first part of this book to help you.

If the expectation involves just me (say, I expect myself to do all the housework needed to have a perfectly clean and decluttered house at all times, no matter what), I explore how realistic that is, for instance, when I am unwell, when I am busy with a large work project, when my husband is at home 24/7 (does your partner dislike hoovering and washing machine noises too?), etc. I usually realise I need to take a compassionate look at my expectations and find a new, more realistic, version, such as "I will keep the house as clean and decluttered as I can as long as it doesn't compromise my health and wellbeing."

If the expectation involves somebody else, I may need to look inside our communication toolbox.

The next step for me is to check whether I have communicated that desire/need to the person involved, in this case, my partner.

Sometimes the answer is "yes, of course! We talked about this 34 years ago when we met", (is it realistic to expect my partner to remember after all these years?) or "yes, of course. We spoke about this very same thing yesterday" (is it realistic to expect my partner to have understood what I meant based on the little time I had to explain what I meant? Is it realistic to expect my partner to remember?) .

Our partners may still be processing that conversation from yesterday, it may well have gone in one ear and out the other, or they may have understood something totally different... On the other hand, we may *think* that we said it clearly, but we may have hinted at it indirectly, as if the other person could fill in the blanks of what we are not saying and hopefully guess correctly. In other words, just because we've said something, it doesn't mean we have communicated it.

We can't control whether another person chooses to or is able to meet our expectation, but in my experience, when I have a chance to voice my expectation clearly, I am more likely to get it met, at least partially or in a different way.

So my recipe for managing my expectations includes a fair amount of clarity and finding the right opportunity to express what I want in just a few, very concrete words, such as "I am very busy this week. Can you handle the washing-up tonight?" When I ask, I also remind myself that the other person is free to say "No" and that I may need to choose between putting up with a messy kitchen or doing the washing up myself regardless.

The positive thing is that I spare myself the feeling of frustration and bitterness that I feel when I expect my husband to know what to do and be ready to run the extra mile, and I don't allow him the freedom to say "No". Assertiveness helps me so that I don't get into judging him as inconsiderate or whatever else my mind might come up with in a moment of disappointment.

EXPLORATION #17: YOUR PARTNER'S SENSE OF SELF (AND/OR YOURS) MAY BE BUILT UPON NEGATIVE EXPERIENCES AND ASSUMPTIONS

We all need validation and reassurance. Due to a difficult past, our partners may have developed a very negative self-image, which may exacerbate our communication problems. For instance, something we mean to be a request may be taken as scathing criticism by them. It is like rubbing salt in an old wound. If we add the fact that they may have made some incorrect assumptions about themselves, such as thinking they were stupid, undesirable, or inadequate, then it is only natural to proceed with caution, compassion, and patience.

Of course, we also have our own past, which may include a fair share of disappointment, misunderstandings, moments

when we were not heard or believed, etc. Therefore slowing down, clarifying things, repeating our message, and trying to understand what our partners are experiencing will be useful strategies to make sure we can both process what is really going on despite the mental noise from past experiences and negative beliefs.

EXPLORATION #18: IF THEY TARGET YOU, IT IS BECAUSE YOU ARE THEIR SAFE PERSON

Have you ever seen a lightning conductor?

I haven't, but I know what they are and I have looked for a photo for us.

Much in the same way as lightning conductors intercept a lightning strike and conduct its electricity safely and predictably to ground, if your partner thinks you are his/her safe person, his/her rock, you will be seen as a safe conductor for their overloads of energy or emotion. It is not personal.

So if during the course of a conversation, they start unloading things on you, remind yourself that it is not personal and, if necessary, check whether they just want to vent or if they would rather have your input. More often than not, they just need to vent.

Much in the same way as a lighting conductor will allow the electric charge to go through it and dissipate into the earth, do what you can to stay grounded (you may choose to press your feet into the ground, or your buttocks into your seat, relax and drop your shoulders, open your chest, etc.), keep breathing and try to breathe from the lower part of your chest...

DON'T TAKE THINGS PERSONALLY

◆ ◆ ◆

EXPLORATION #19: GIVE THEM THE FACTS, PLEASE!

I am a very emotional person and I LOVE words, so when I talk to friends I get to talk freely about my feelings, thoughts, emotions, etc.

THANK YOU, GUYS! WHERE WOULD I BE WITHOUT MY DEAR FRIENDS???

I can use lots and lots of words, and they continue listening.

Amazing!

Now, with our partners, the situation is different. We need to focus on the data and forget about everything else. If we fail to remember to do that, they might get confused and take the first word that reaches their brain and go on a tangent. (By the way, they don't do it on purpose to derail the conversation. They are working with what they have heard and their intention is probably to keep the conversation going. Most probably because they know how much we value communication! If you have never seen it this way, I would love to see your face right now! Don't worry. This penny has just dropped for me too!).

EXPLORATION #20: TRANSITIONS TAKE TIME AND PREPARATION

As we have already explored, changes take time because they involve a process of rebuilding how our partners make sense of their experience as a whole. Transitions are needed before changes.

One of such daily changes is from whatever my husband is doing to having a meal. It seems to help him to have a very fixed routine and a huge clock in front of him. There are days when I realise he is in the middle of something, so I check whether I should delay the meal somehow. He may need more than one reminder. He rarely minds if I remind him that it is time to stop and eat and then leave him alone.

GIVE LOTS OF REMINDERS BEFORE TRANSITIONS

◆ ◆ ◆

EXPLORATION #21: DECLARATIVE LANGUAGE

Have you ever asked your partner to do something and it didn't go down well? Did you keep insisting, only to feel exhausted after your words seemed to be falling on deaf ears?

Sometimes, our partners may also think we are infringing on their *autonomy*, when we are simply trying to connect with them through communication.

It is generally useful to avoid giving orders, making direct requests or asking direct questions that contain the expectation for a specific behaviour. This is because it reduces your partner's control and will be perceived as a threat, leading to behaviours such as yelling, throwing things, sarcasm, changing the subject, not answering at all, shutting eyes, physical ailments, ignoring, blaming and criticising you, etc.

Instead, it is better to use declarative language, that is to say, make statements, comments or observations or phrase things in such a way that they do not involve your partner and instead refer to an object, yourself, or other people.

Declarative language is a way to make it impersonal (or not about them). For instance, instead of asking our partners to take the rubbish out, we can say that the rubbish needs taking out.

I know that this doesn't work with everybody, so we can also ask

USE DECLARATIVE (NOT IMPERATIVE) LANGUAGE

them whether they prefer to do the dishes or to take the rubbish out.

Some people suggest that when our partners refuse to cooperate, we could try modelling the behaviour we want to see or leave visible clues around for them to process in their own time. The modelling doesn't seem to work for us. I end up doing the whole thing while he is watching and telling me how to do it better. Leaving clues seems to work better. For instance, a couple of weeks ago my computer broke down and he lent me his PC, which meant I was working from his home office instead of mine. While I was there, I grabbed a piece of paper and jotted things down on our to-do list. One of the things was changing the shower filter (he likes having a shower head that sends out a thin spray of filtered water, so a few years ago I bought him one for his birthday. I also bought some replacement cartridges, but he forgets to change them). I also added a few things he needs to do himself and left the list on his desk To my amazement, he has not mentioned the list since, but has done something and crossed it off! Wow!

◆ ◆ ◆

EXPLORATION #22: LIVING IN BLACK AND WHITE

Your partner may have a polarised, inflexible way of seeing the world. If your partner sees things as either good or bad and people as friends or foes, you will know it soon enough.

I suspect that one of the factors of this black-and-white thinking without any gray in between is perfectionism. Whatever they do has to be perfect, otherwise it is a disaster which is not worth doing or presenting to the world. They may excel at tasks where they can see they are succeeding but fail at even simpler tasks if they can't see a "right" or "wrong" way of doing it.

No wonder relationships are not usually on their priority list!

No wonder they try to evade anything that has an emotional charge attached to it!

How can we ever get relationships or emotions perfectly right?

Unfortunately, our partners can extend their striving for perfection to us as well. They may set standards of perfection on everything we do, offering "constructive criticism" to help us get it right (according to their standards, their values, their blueprint, their expectations…).

This perfectionism creates a distance between us and our partners, generating obstacles in our communication. It also makes it difficult for our partners to stop improving on something when it is good enough but not perfect in their eyes, unless they are sure they can come to continue improving it later on.

One thing that may work for us, dear reader, is to model making mistakes for them and be OK with it, accepting imperfection calmly or getting things good enough for now and improving on them with time.

This is a tricky one to navigate. We tend to resort to humour at home and I am finding excellent results from just allowing him plenty of time and space to process.

EXPLORATION #23: ONLY ONE RAILTRACK

What happens when there is only one rail track? Well, if one train is going in one direction, it cannot take another track and it is not possible for another train to come the other way.

It may be useful to imagine that our partner's brain capacity is like that. Once they get going, they keep going in that direction… because there is no other option for them. Even if a landslide has blocked the track, they will still go forwards and crash against the same obstacles over and over.

In other words, they may not only have difficulty coming up with a plan B, they may also fail to see that a plan B is possible at all. I guess plan B feels to them like getting derailed.

If we confront them, we may experience something similar to two trains crashing head on!

If it is necessary to get them to change direction, we may need to wait until they realise that the track they are on is not getting them where they want to go, and they themselves attempt another way or ask for help.

Sometimes, the same happens in conversation. Our partners may divert the conversation to something that is interesting for them and then go on and on and on and on, without realising how that is affecting everybody else. I would describe this as once they grab the microphone, they won't let go! I sometimes imagine that my husband is like a football player running with the ball beyond the boundaries of the field, who keeps running and running off site, instead of playing the game. It makes me laugh. Sometimes I share this with my husband and he laughs, too. Sometimes, he sees me laughing and he realises he has gone off-site.

In order to ease our own conversations, my husband and I are experimenting with turn-taking. I have suggested allowing the other person to say 3 statements before grabbing the mike back. My husband suggested counting the statements with our fingers. I thought he meant each speaker would count to make the other person aware of what was going on. Then I saw he was counting **my** statements, too. OK, less work for me. Then he said "3 statements minimum"... so I think we are not there yet, but he is getting the concept of turn-taking now, which he didn't get earlier, so there is definite progress.

If I model reciprocity and listen until my husband has finished a point, then I have more chances of him doing the same for me. We have had quite a few conversations about the difference between reciprocity and interruption, too.

EXPLORATION #24: "NO" IS A FOUR-LETTER WORD

AVOID SAYING "NO" (SUGGEST, INVITE...)

Some words such as "no", "don't", "can't", "must" or "have to" convey ways to do or not do things. In other words, they lay the rules for right and wrong action. Much in the same way as imperative language, they may be perceived as impositions which impinge on *autonomy*, so they can be triggering and elicit a negative reaction. It is better to try to avoid them as much as possible, while maintaining an element of choice and handing control to our partners.

For instance, instead of saying "No" to a request, we can say "I'd love to, but it is not possible today because... We could try tomorrow. In the meantime, would you like to .... or...?"

◆ ◆ ◆

EXPLORATION #25: IT IS BETTER TO SAY WHAT YOU MEAN CLEARLY

Do you remember what we reflected on in EXPLORATION #8?

JUST BECAUSE SOMEBODY IS GOOD AT TALKING, IT DOESN'T MEAN THEY ARE EQUALLY GOOD AT LISTENING

When I met my husband we were both teachers. We were teaching different age groups and in different contexts, and the subject matters were different, too. Our passion for teaching, however, seemed to be on par with each other's. He would lecture for hours without need for notes or any prompts. He would handle questions with such confidence and depth of knowledge that I was in awe. So I didn't realise that when people asked him questions, he would come up with impressive answers that bore no relation to the questions. It was only years later that he told me he had memorised the whole thing.

So his impressive deliveries were not based on his mastery of language or of the subject matter. In his case, they were based on memory. I am not suggesting this is a general rule. I am just sharing this experience as a reminder that we may misjudge our partner's cognitive and communicative skills because they may have adopted very ingenious adaptations. I have learned, for instance, that it is not unusual for people on the spectrum to borrow ready-made phrases and use them as scripts for their everyday conversations. They may rehash things they have heard on TV, films, or on the radio, or things they have read somewhere.

If I want to give communication a chance, then, firstly, I need to be clear about what I want to say before I start speaking and whether it is worth mentioning at all. Remember the traffic light system I suggested at the beginning of Part Two:

Not important at all. Stop!

Not so important. Wait or proceed with caution.

Important enough for me or the relationship. We might need to schedule a good time for both.

I really cherish conversations with friends in which we may speak about something in order to find clarity. We can brainstorm together and at the end we find a deeper truth. I can rarely do that with my husband. It is exhausting. It is confusing. It is frustrating (and perhaps, pointless?) for him.

So when I speak to my husband I need to have some sort of an intention for opening my mouth and I need to express it in short, to the point, sentences. Clarity must be the starting point with him, not the destination we get to after sharing a discovery process.

My husband also reminds me that he can't understand poetry or "meaningless polite sounds". All these "flowery expressions" (that's what my husband calls them) mean nothing to him. He can't put the pieces of the linguistic puzzle together in his head because there are too many pieces to consider. So I need to be mindful of my use of language in that sense too. It has to be something concrete and not invoke too many images or he will stick to one and go on a tangent. (Between you and me, that is the end of a conversation for me when he does that!!!)

In many instances, if you don't pay close attention you may miss the issue because your partner may continue to hold a reasonably logical conversation. However, on closer inspection, your partner may be speaking, but their message may not match the conversation at all. Alternatively, the conversation may have moved on and they come back to an earlier point, or they may even talk non-stop (*because when they speak, they have control of the conversation and they don't have to exert themselves as much as when they are listening*). This may puzzle many people. They may hear your partner talk at length about complex matters and they (we?) may not realise how much your partner may struggle to receive messages from others (and on top of that, to try to remember them!)

If any of this sounds familiar, perhaps you would need to start developing your own strategy: create mind maps, discuss the topic with other people before speaking to your partner, blog, speak to your therapist, and write poetry/songs, etc. before speaking to your partner.

BONUS REMINDERS: Remember that...

1) Check how you show up. If your behaviour is not consistently transmitting the message you want your partner to get, you are not saying what you mean.

Of course, communication is two-way. Your partner's behaviour is also communicating important messages.

Let me share a recent personal example to illustrate what I mean. About a month ago, my cousins invited me to join them for a week in Spain. They both live in Argentina and we haven't seen one another for years. My heart said a big YES! I was ill with Covid-19 at the time, but there was plenty of time for me to recover before the trip. I checked with my husband and he said "of course you must go. You really want to see them and it is a great opportunity." I booked my flights, the train tickets in Spain, and also made some hotel bookings. My cousins made some of the reservations for the three of us from their end. When I recovered from Covid-19, my husband was still keeping very much to himself. We normally hold hands, kiss, speak a bit, or keep physical contact during the day, but there was none of that. He was still keeping to himself in his home office, barely speaking to me, keeping physically distant. At night he would get into bed, turn his back to me and not even say goodnight. He was eating very little. I thought that perhaps he was taking his time to transition back from the Covid-19 protocol to our normal routines. However, I needed to cancel the trip to Spain. It was a heart-wrenching decision. I told my cousins (who were very gracious about it) and then I told my husband before going to bed one night. The next morning, it was as if he had flicked an internal switch and become his usual self. He asked me for my hand, he kissed me, he talked to me again. He started smiling again. He started eating more and seemed to enjoy his food again.

Looking back, I wonder whether I got his previous behaviour wrong. Was his behaviour saying he didn't really want me to go to Spain? I think that is very likely. Most probably he was worried because he is starting to run his own online retail business and that is taking all his waking hours. I wonder whether he was worried because he knew that at the very least he would have had to cook for himself (he won't have ready-made or processed meals) and he would have had to get his own smartphone, because I would have taken mine with me. Who knows?

2) As neurotypicals, we not only listen to what is said (the linguistic content), but also scan the situation for other clues, such as body language, which words are being emphasised, intonation, the volume of the voice, repetitions, how high or low the tone of the voice is, whether the person speaks in a monotone or whether they modulate the tone according to their intended meaning, etc. All this second group of clues are usually called paralinguistic features. When our neurodiverse partner doesn't "transmit" such paralinguistic information or

when they transmit it in a different way from which we are used to, **our brain subconsciously fills in the blanks**, giving rise to many misunderstandings about the intended meaning of interactions. How many times do we get offended by what our partners/ spouses intended as a totally innocent statement of something they noticed?

EXPLORATION #26: LONG STRINGS OF VERBAL INFORMATION DON'T HELP

My husband has explained to me that when people speak, if sentences are too long, he may only get the beginning and the end, which may not make sense or which may make up a totally different, distorted message in his head. We started talking about this while we were watching videos. He would ask me to rewind and replay things several times and I could see him trying to build up the complete meaning.

When he was listening to a scientist he admires, he would get lost in every sentence, because my husband perceived the speech as a long string of adjectives and adverbs one after the other that didn't make any sense.

He usually prefers written material so that he can go over it several times, which is good to know because it helps our relationship. There is a limit to the number of times I can hear the same sentence over and over and over again on a topic I am not interested in!

When people speak, your partner may have to work out

the intended message, which may be laborious and time-consuming. That is why, I guess, they shut down and don't speak when they are exhausted. They have no more energy for "verbal gymnastics".

GIVE PLENTY OF TIME TO PROCESS INFORMATION

Some couple therapists suggest keeping our exchanges to 3 sentences and then checking that the message has been received accurately.

Sometimes I look at my husband and I can see in his face that he is still processing what I have said, as if he were playing the message in slow motion in his head, so I stop talking and if he doesn't give me a cue to continue, I check whether I have the green light to go on or whether I need to repeat something.

Sometimes it takes more than 3 attempts for a message to go through. Sometimes when I check, he just got the beginning and the end.

It helps him when I utter short sentences, raise my voice and pitch a bit (as if I were angry, which may perhaps explain why he looks relieved, almost pleased, when I raise my voice in anger), and leave generous gaps in between (Do you remember the 8 second pause from EXPLORATION #6?)

EXPLORATION #27: TOP-DOWN AND BOTTOM-UP THINKING

Some people, like me, can hear something and imagine examples, that is to say, we have no problem with top-down thinking. For instance, we may hear a rule and see the different contexts to which we can apply it.

The first time I encountered the concept of "bottom-up thinking" was during some training with Dr Temple Grandin. People on the autism spectrum follow a different path when they think. Some of them need to explore every single possible instance before arriving at the rule.

Sometimes it is painful for us to wait for them to finish processing all the examples and double-checking there is no more data that contradicts the rule. I experience this when we are shopping. My husband has to check and double-check the features, the price, and every single detail before even comparing products, by which time I have lost the will to buy anything, but I am digressing...

In other words, **people on the autistic spectrum tend to take in the details *before* discovering the concept behind them**. Imagine that! Your partner's autistic mind is processing an enormous amount of fragments of data before being able to arrive at a hypothesis that explains all of them. No wonder they get sensory overload! It must be confusing and tiring to get those unconnected fragments and try to fit the pieces of the puzzle together.

A neurotypical brain processes the different pieces automatically according to previous rules or learning. It is as if we compare the new data to the rules we have in our memory, which, of course, makes the process much faster.

I am not saying one is better than the other. From what I have experienced, the autistic mind is more thorough, the non-autistic mind is faster.

This difference has huge repercussions in communication. When we come to our partners because we want to share some exciting news, we may be met with lots of questions about details that seem irrelevant to us. This happens very often to my husband and me and I am still learning. I am still trying to remember that he doesn't do it to stop me talking because he is not interested. Quite the opposite, he is interested. He is trying to put the pieces together. He NEEDS the pieces in order to get the whole picture!

On the other hand, this trait means that the autistic mind is great at coming up with out-of-the-box ideas, because in their bottom-up thinking approach, they may be better at reorganising information in a novel way.

On the downside, because each detail is essential for them to make meaning out of life, when one detail changes, their whole world collapses. I understand this like a person who has been creating a very intricate 3D sand sculpture for hours and once it is finished, we move a bit of sand from underneath and the whole thing collapses (this is linked to what we talked about on EXPLORATION #11 Any change destroys the whole).

Let's not go stomping on their sandcastles if we can avoid it!

P.S. If your partner is anything like mine, any little change (especially when it affects his routine) may seem much worse than stomping on his sandcastle. It seems to inflict such deep pain and to create such chaos for him that he reacts as if I were trying to introduce a change in his genetic make-up. It seems to go very deep for him. It may be something that is totally insignificant for me, such as saying something to him when he expects silence because he is on his morning routine and needs to go from A to B to C. Just saying something that shifts his attention from the routine to my words is enough to cause chaos and irritation.

I can't prevent this from happening all the time. When things like this happen, I leave my husband alone as soon as I can so that he can (in time) resume his routine.

EXPLORATION #28:
SPECIAL INTEREST(S)

Special interests are a kind of blissful bubble where the problems of everyday life don't exist, a way of blocking intrusive or unpleasant thoughts or feelings. Trying to remove them is like destroying their lifeline.

When my husband starts spending more and more time on his special interest, which seems to change from time to time, I look for any possible reasons. Have there been any recent or impending changes? Is there anything that may be increasing any sensory or food sensitivities? Is there anything that may be increasing his anxiety? Is he sleeping well? Am I experiencing any of these myself and as a consequence he is using his special interest because he doesn't know how to deal with my emotions/help me?

The answers to these questions will usually help me unlock any barriers to communication. If we can work on what is causing his increased need for his special interest, I may get a green light for communication. Otherwise, I may need to allow him plenty of solitude for a while.

EXPLORATION #29: DON'T MAKE THEM UNCOMFORTABLE!

Much in the same way as our partners don't like being made uncomfortable in any way, talking about certain topics may make them run a mile. This is especially the case if the topic is related to the division of chores in the house or things you would like to improve in the relationship. Do you know what I am talking about?

It is good to be aware of which topics make our partners uncomfortable, and to take time to plan our conversations around those. We may need to prepare some bullet points to keep us focussed and objective. We may need to find a way to make the topic lighter for them by adding examples or elements from their special interest.

We will certainly need to reassure them that they haven't done anything wrong.

Ideally, we would schedule the conversation well ahead and tell our partners what the topic is and what the timeframe will be.

If it is a really uncomfortable topic for them, they will try to avoid the conversation. Sometimes there is no alternative but to reschedule.

EXPLORATION #30: ONLY INTERESTING THINGS, PLEASE

We all have our preferences; however, we are usually capable of extending our fields of interest to include what other people are interested in. In the case of people like our partners, this interest seems to be limited to what is personally interesting to them.

There is something that we can perhaps learn from our partners: sometimes they may engage with us in conversation as a bridge (which feels more like a wedge, really) to start talking about what really interests them. We can, in turn, use things we know they are interested in as a bridge towards another topic or back into the conversation we thought we were having.

In a way, I think this goes together with the previous exploration, but I broke it down to make it easier to metabolise.

It is helpful, therefore, for us to find ways of making what we are talking about comfortable (for instance, by making it more impersonal, factual, non-blaming) and interesting in their eyes (for instance, by relating it to their own experience or special interests).

I have found this exploration has spared us many verbal battles!

EXPLORATION #31: COLOUR CODES

As we have explored, communication doesn't need to be verbal all the time. If you have a visual partner, perhaps you can explore using something, such as a coloured card, to convey messages. For example, RED may be for "Danger. I am upset and I need time alone." ORANGE may be for "I am getting a bit stressed". YELLOW may mean "I am not sure what you mean." BLACK may be for "I am upset and I welcome your support/a hug/your input/your help." Of course, it needs to be a shared code and it is much better if your partner is the one who allocates most if not all of the meanings for the colours because they will be easier to remember as they will follow your partner's logic.

There is no point in sending messages if our partners don't know what the colours mean, or if the decoding process is too stressful for them. However, if used sparingly, especially during a conversation that doesn't seem to be flowing easily, colours can be a quick way to express/understand which the best way forward is.

EXPLORATION #32: SELECTIVE BRAIN FUNCTIONING

If you have ever had a long conversation with your partner which ended up in an agreement and then you found out that for him/her it was as if it had never happened at all, I hope you will find some peace here.

Let's oversimplify things and say that human beings have 2 kinds of memory: short-term memory and long-term memory. Short-term memory is a bit like the RAM in our computer, it stores the information we need for the tasks in hand. In the case of the computer, we can then choose to save that information on the hard drive, or we can discard it. A similar process takes place in our brains: we have some information in our short-term memory for a while and then our mental processing decides whether it will discard it or store it in our long-term memory. Sometimes we can make a conscious effort to store something in our long-term memory (such as when we are studying) but in general, this is an automatic process.

A person on the autism spectrum may have a slightly different process in that their short-term memory might be equally efficient, but then the process of selecting whether to store or discard the information may have some issues. Some of the information that would be good to store, for example, ends up in the bin lost forever or, at best, left in a corner, unsorted, covered by other things, and difficult to retrieve unless they make a huge effort and get plenty of reminders and prompts.

In other words, our partners may have problems with storing information in their long-term memory. They are not kidding, they are not doing it on purpose, they are not gaslighting us. They have what we may call "selective memory".

My husband calls me "his external hard drive", and he may be right to some extent. In general, I seem to have more available space in my long-term memory than him.

It is sometimes puzzling that the same people who are capable of remembering an enormous amount of information when it comes to their special interests may struggle to remember how to make a soup. That, however, is one of the distinctive features of autism. Some people describe this mental functioning as "spiky" because in some aspects it may excel and in others it may be low.

The great news is that people on the spectrum can use technology (or notes) to remind themselves of important things. We can also help them by writing down important information for them (some people use text messages or emails, what works for us is a large visible sign on paper).

If the issue for them is to remember where they put things, it may help them if they use their tendency to sort and line things up to decide where each thing belongs, and to remind them to put things back "home" when they have finished using them.

Mind you, sometimes we need to scaffold their memory further. For example, yesterday my husband was looking for some adhesive to fix something. He is very meticulous about where he puts his tools and stuff, so I don't interfere. He was going around the house looking for it everywhere, the clock was ticking, and he was getting grumpy. I asked him whether he had looked in the usual place where he stores it. He said "I used it the other day for such and such. I don't know where I left it." I waited a bit and then asked again: "Have you looked where you normally keep it?" and I left him at it. Later on I asked him whether he had found it and he said he had. I asked him where it was and he seemed surprised when he announced: "You were right. It was in its usual place."

I think what worked was that I told him and left him alone. Insisting tends to create a lot of resistance and it doesn't end well at home.

◆ ◆ ◆

I truly hope the exploration on communication pays off for you, your partner and your relationship.

Remember to remain as curious, calm and non-judgemental (towards yourself and towards your partner) as you can.

If you are experiencing specific problems due to the way your partner speaks or understands language, I would highly recommend the book by Olga Bogdashina, *Communication issues in autism and Asperger syndrome*, where you will find a thorough discussion of theories of language learning, cognitive styles and functions in autism, and language peculiarities such as echolalia, pronoun reversal, extreme literalness, metaphorical language, neologisms, affirmation by repetition, repetitive questioning, and poor control of prosody, among others. To give you an idea of the gems you may find in this book, I would like to mention the concept of language as 'stress reliever', which I have seen many times in my partner, but I had never heard of before. Olga Bogdashina states that "In stressful situations autistic people may talk to themselves in order to 'unwind'" (Bogdashina, 2005). Prof. Tony Attwood has said that they sometimes talk to themselves in an attempt to slow down thought. It is great to know that!

◆ ◆ ◆

I'll Meet You There

I am sure that if you and I were sitting together, we would have lots to continue exploring. We might even share some deep longings and some deep feelings.

I am honoured to have travelled this far with you and I am confident you will find your unique way of following your own wisdom.

◆ ◆ ◆

Just to summarise our journey together, what we have actually done is moved from suffering to responsibility and power:

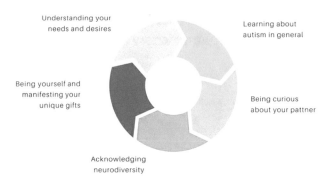

The move from suffering to responsibility and power

Understanding your needs and desires

Learning about autism in general

Being yourself and manifesting your unique gifts

Being curious about your pattner

Acknowledging neurodiversity

❖ ❖ ❖

There is one more place I would like to visit with you.

We have explored a few areas of your life together, we have explored aspects of communication that may be present in your relationship, but there is still vast land that we haven't explored, the land of "I don't know".

Sometimes we experience things that escape our understanding. Some of those experiences may be puzzling beyond comprehension, others may be heart-wrenching, still others may be thrilling moments of joy. Whatever the flavour of the experience, if we don't resist it and we don't insist on understanding it either, we seem to touch on a different mindspace or state of consciousness.

It is that mindspace where the only thing to do is be with the experience as it is, not knowing why it is happening, not knowing how to respond, and not knowing what to do next.

It is that space where we can only watch in vulnerability and innocence, while we wonder at the truth of what is going on.

It is a space that rather than contracting us, makes us feel lighter and more expanded.

Perhaps one of us will then say "I don't know..." and the other one will hopefully reply "I don't know either, but here I am."

Below is some marriage advice from 1886. I hope you will feel inspired by it.

Marriage Advice

Let your love be stronger than your hate or anger.

Learn the wisdom of compromise, for it is better to bend a little than to break.

Believe the best rather than the worst.

People have a way of living up or down to your opinion of them.

Remember that true friendship is the basis for any lasting relationship. The person you choose to marry is deserving of the courtesies and kindnesses you bestow on your friends.

Please hand this down to your children and your children's children: The more things change the more they are the same.

Jane Wells (1886)

THE HAPPY ENDING YOU HAVE BEEN EXPECTING

In our movie, there is no happy ending, just happy new beginnings each day. My husband is very handsome, funny (have you read the "About the Author" section that he wrote about me?), compassionate, passionate, stubborn, innovative...

We also seem to be opposites in every way, which many people we know find hilarious!

I have recently found the perfect analogy to describe us. You may have heard 'The Hummingbird and the Elephant' fable. I have heard Paul Micallef (from "Asperger's from the Inside") refer to himself and his wife by analogy to an elephant and a hummingbird. My husband and I agree that that image describes us, too!

You see? My husband takes his time to consider things before making any decision and then double-checks a million times (he says I exaggerate) before taking the next step. Answers and ideas come to him in bits, so he needs time to put things together. He has lots of stamina and, if he is interested in something or if he has a personal motivation to do it, he can go on and on and on for hours, days, months, years! He thrives when things remain stable. He needs to do things in his own time. He has fewer interests than me. He doesn't thrive when there are too many options, probably because he needs to explore them in detail (I almost typed "in excruciatingly painful" detail, but that is my perception, not his reality). When he is going in one direction, he tends to keep going in that direction.

I normally decide very fast. Answers and ideas just come to me as complete wholes. I have a fair amount of stamina but I give everything 110% of my attention and energy, so I may run out of energy faster than my husband. I need to take breaks. I thrive when I have new things to learn and discover. I need structure but I also love variety. I have lots of interests. There is never enough time for me to do everything I would like to do. I don't mind having lots of options because, in general, it is easy for me to establish priorities and to shortlist just a few options. I can change direction more easily than my husband and I seem to have a wider range of directions than him. I think my husband will also say that, much like hummingbirds, I am noisy. I like connecting to people, especially through words, deep conversations, and emotions.

I like this imagery very much because it helps us celebrate our own features and strengths. I hope you will like the drawing I have created to illustrate this.

The elephant had to be cute and have big eyes. I love my husband's big brown eyes!

He never fails to surprise me.

When I think he has come to a dead end, he will find a way round it.

When everybody thinks it can't be done, he will find a way, an out-of-the-box, low budget, genius way.

As a last reminder, try to remember that whatever your spouse/partner says or does makes total sense to them, so try to find out what it could mean. Look for their patterns and try to speak to their intention, not their performance. People on the spectrum separate intention from behaviour. They know their intention (e.g. to express love) but they can't see how you feel, how you need to hear it. They just think that because they mean well, that should be good enough.

My wish for you is that instead of a happy ending, you may also find many happy new beginnings.

LET'S STAY CONNECTED

Let's continue the conversation online. If you would be interested in joining an online forum to share your experience with regards to the activities and ideas presented in Resilient Loving and The Companion, and perhaps any additional situations you may be going through, please email me at mabel@resilientloving.co.uk. I understand privacy is very important, so our forum will not be visible to non-members and you will be able to use any nickname you want when you register.

You may also read and comment on Resilient Loving blog (https://resilientloving.blogspot.com/)

If you have found this book useful, I would like to encourage you to write a Review on Amazon. You can also help me to spread the word on social media. Thank you!

FURTHER RESOURCES THAT YOU MAY WANT TO EXPLORE

(UK-based unless specified)

The National Autistic Society

http://www.autism.org.uk

Peer Support Group for Spouses/Partners of Adults with Autism

https://www.meetup.com/Support-Group-for-NT-partners/

Family rights groups

http://www.frg.org.uk

Family Lives: helpline as well as useful information

0808 800 2222

askus@familylives,org.uk

http://www.familylives.org.uk

Action for Asperger's (not-for-profit organisation from CORBY, NORTHAMPTONSHIRE):

01536 266681

https://www.actionforaspergers.org

Different Together Facebook group:

https://www.facebook.com/groups/differenttogether

Living Well with Autism (Derbyshire)

0808 178 9363

https://www.livingwellwithautism.org.uk/

Domestic violence - If you feel you are in danger you can contact:

Refuge Freephone Helpline

0808 2000 247

https://www.nationaldahelpline.org.uk

Samaritans

116 123

Asperger/Autism Network (AANE) (USA) offers a free discussion forum and open and closed groups. For more information, visit:

https://www.aane.org/resources/adults/support-social-groups-couples-partners/#online-discussion-forum-sp

Prof. Tony Attwood's site (AUSTRALIA):

https://tonyattwood.com.au/

Prof. Tony Attwood and Dr. Michelle Garnett's site (AUSTRALIA):

attwoodandgarnettevents.com/

Hendrickx Associates
Diagnosis, coaching, counselling, training

https://www.asperger-training.com/

Text SHOUT to 85258

https://giveusashout.org/

If you are feeling anxious/worried/stressed get help from a crisis volunteer 24/7.

National Suicide Prevention Helpline UK

0800 689 5652

https://www.spbristol.org/

Other groups:

https://www.healingcassandra.com/

(US-based)

https://www.aane.org/

(US-based)
https://www.neurodiverselove.com/general-7-1

(US-based)

https://www.adultaspergerschat.com/2019/07/skype-counseling-for-struggling-couples.html

(US-based, with Marc Hutten)

https://www.meetup.com/asperger-syndrome-partners-family-of-adults-with-asd/
(US-based, with Dr Kathy Marshack)

An online community for neurodiverse relationships:

https://www.lovingdifference.net/

REFERENCES

Bogdashina, O., 2005. *Communication issues in autism and Asperger syndrome*. London: Jessica Kingsley Publishers.

Brown, B., 2021. *Atlas of the heart: Mapping meaningful connection and the language of human experience*, London, Vermilion

Dass, R. and Gorman, P., 2001. *How can I help?*. Alfred A. Knopf: New York, p.139.

Festinger, L., 1957. *A Theory of cognitive dissonance*. Stanford, CA: Stanford University Press

Frankel, Viktor E., 2004. *Man's Search for Meaning*, Croydon, Rider Books

Sunderland M. and Armstrong, N., 2018. *The Emotion Cards*. Oxon: Routledge

❖ ❖ ❖

ABOUT THE AUTHOR

(In her husband's words in 2022.
He's also taken the photo)

We have known each other for 34 years and have been married for 32 years. Mabel is an unfathomable mystery that up to now I can't get to know.

She has been incredibly patient with me. While she was doing a teaching course at college several years ago, she heard for the first time about Asperger's. The symptoms described by the tutor were very similar to my behaviour. When she started reading the symptoms to me, I said "Yes, this is me. Yes, I do this." Since then, Mabel started to do an incredible amount of self-study about Asperger's and autism, buying a lot of books, watching a lot of videos on YouTube or whatever and after that doing counselling courses and she went so far as to contact the world's expert in Asperger's and autism.

She slowly started to introduce me to autism. As I am a bit slow reading, she digested all those mountains of information and summarised them for me. In the beginning I didn't pay much attention to her endeavour to improve the relationship and make it better. With time, I have been appreciating more and more all her efforts as it has produced a remarkable improvement in the relationship. It doesn't mean that we reached the ideal concept of marriage, but things got much better with the years and the key point has been the fact that we understood how different we are and how we can find a middle point where both can be reasonably comfortable, sparing us lots of arguments and misunderstandings.

She is a good cook.

She is patient except when I ask her to repeat the same thing twice.

SPECIAL THANKS

Wow! I didn't expect to get so emotional in this section.

Mabel, come on! This is not an acceptance speech at the Academy Awards ceremony!

There are so many people that come to mind but firstly, I would like to thank my loyal laptop, which one day got a shock when the switch in the socket the laptop was connected to was off and after the battery charge ran out, it gave out a horrible Piff! and stopped working for a week, keeping the latest version of this book (my baby) locked inside it. Before you ask, yes, I did have backups, of course, but not for the last few edits (long story). So thank you, laptop for being well again and allowing me to carry on working and backing things up properly.

Special thanks to my late father for his great memory and sense of humour, and to my late mother for her dedication to keeping the family together and her love of music... and chocolate. Special thanks to Claudio, my big brother, who is always surprising and inspiring me, no matter what challenges life throws at him. Special thanks to my late uncle, for calling me "daughter" and treating me as if I were another daughter, too. Special thanks to my two nieces, my two nephews, my two dear cousins and my newly-born grandniece for all the joy they bring into my life. Special thanks to my late great grandmother, who paid for my education and private lessons so that I could learn English and make my wish to become a teacher come true. Special thanks to my grandparents, all four of whom taught me to be resilient and to keep going.

Special thanks to my friends, both those who support my dreams and those who question them. There are 3 main friends whom I would like to thank especially (ladies first). Firstly, my friend/dream-supporter and Sunday morning confidante, who always listens empathically, prays for our wellbeing, nudges me to see my therapist, and comes up with wise insights. Then, I would like to thank my life-long friend, who always picks me up on my way down and also challenges my perceptions with different perspectives. She has a great capacity for sensing what I am missing and asking meaningful questions. Last, but not least, I would like to thank my supportive, patient, and caring friend (and his dog) for sharing so much during the past 30 years or so, for showing me my power while seeing my vulnerability, and for always finding the perfect flowers for any occasion! All three of them have been with me for years. All three of them have seen me really down… and they stayed, they held me and they helped me stand up again. Thank you!

Special thanks to Keith for making a very strong case that it was in my best interest to get my draft book reviewed by a native speaker of English.

Special thanks to Mandy Pearson, therapist/copyeditor/ cheerleader/"magic-worker", who has done a wonderful job understanding what I wanted to achieve, checking that my Spanish thinking doesn't interfere with my writing, and suggesting great new ideas to take my book to a different level. It has been such a pleasure and inspiration to read your enthusiastic feedback and to meet over Zoom to discuss details and new dreams!

Special thanks to the therapists who have listened to my rants and led me to new insights and a bit of growth (I hope!). So many times, I still remember what they said many years later and it still makes sense, or the penny finally drops.

I would also like to thank all those people who have taught me about autism… or anything else.

Special thanks to Dr. Tony Attwood and Dr. Michelle Garnett (as well as her PA Beverlee) whom I admire and who always help me find a positive way of dealing with a painful situation. Thank you all of you (or whoever is responsible) for introducing me to the music from Gypsy & The Cat during live training events, and above all for making it possible for me to start to have a better understanding of my husband and our relationship. I truly admire you (yes, I know I have already said so, but it is so true!) and I can't even begin to articulate how deep my gratitude is for being able to learn from your knowledge and experience in such a relatable manner.

Special thanks to Different Together CIC (and Jo) for all the work they carried out to raise awareness and support our kind of relationships. I always wonder where I would be without my support group!

So… huge thanks to everybody on the Meetup Peer Support Group for Spouses/Partners of Adults with Autism, who touch my heart with their care, insights, support, humour, vulnerability and lived experiences.

And of course, my most special thanks to my husband, who has been very patient with me despite our differences, who never ceases to amaze me with out-of-the-box thinking and his own ways of demonstrating love. Thank you for writing the About the Author section and for taking such a lovely photo, too.

Last, but in no way least, thank you, dear reader, for being brave and coming on this journey with me and so many others, for trusting me, and above all for trusting your own wisdom to face what may be happening in your life.

Made in United States
Troutdale, OR
12/06/2024